Genuine Intellectuals
Academic and Social Responsibilities
of Universities in Africa

Bernard Nsokika Fonlon

Langaa Research & Publishing CIG
Mankon, Bamenda

Publisher:
Langaa RPCIG
Langaa Research & Publishing Common Initiative
Group
P.O. Box 902 Mankon
Bamenda
North West Region
Cameroon
Langaagrp@gmail.com
www.langaa-rpcig.net

Distributed outside N. America by African Books
Collective
orders@africanbookscollective.com
www.africanbookscollective.com

Distributed in N. America by Michigan State University Press
msupress@msu.edu
www.msupress.msu.edu

ISBN: 9956-558-59-1

© Bernard Nsokika Fonlon 2009
Previously published with the titles:
To Every African Freshman or the Nature, End and
Purpose of University Studies - 1969
The Genuine Intellectual - 1978

DISCLAIMER

All views expressed in this publication are those of the author and do not necessarily reflect the views of Langaa RPCIG.

Titles by *Langaa* RPCIG

Francis B. Nyamnjoh
Stories from Abakwa
Mind Searching
The Disillusioned African
The Convert
Souls Forgotten
Married But Available

Dibussi Tande
No Turning Back: Poems of Freedom 1990-1993
Scribbles from the Den: Essays on Politics and Collective Memory in Cameroon

Kangsen Feka Wakai
Fragmented Melodies

Ntemfac Ofege
Namondo: Child of the Water Spirits
Hot Water for the Famous Seven

Emmanuel Fru Doh
Not Yet Damascus
The Fire Within
Africa's Political Wastelands: The Bastardization of Cameroon
Oriki'badan
Wading the Tide

Thomas Jing
Tale of an African Woman

Peter Wuteh Vakunta
Grassfields Stories from Cameroon
Green Rape: Poetry for the Environment
Majunga Tok: Poems in Pidgin English
Cry, My Beloved Africa
No Love Lost
Straddling The Mungo: A Book of Poems in English & French

Ba'bila Mutia
Coils of Mortal Flesh

Kehbuma Langmia
Titabet and the Takumbeng
An Evil Meal of Evil

Victor Elame Musinga
The Barn
The Tragedy of Mr. No Balance

Ngessimo Mathe Mutaka
Building Capacity: Using TEFL and African Languages as Development-oriented Literacy Tools

Milton Krieger
Cameroon's Social Democratic Front: Its History and Prospects as an Opposition Political Party, 1990-2011

Sammy Oke Akombi
The Raped Amulet
The Woman Who Ate Python
Beware the Drives: Book of Verse
The Wages of Corruption

Susan Nkwentie Nde
Precipice
Second Engagement

Francis B. Nyamnjoh & Richard Fonteh Akum
The Cameroon GCE Crisis: A Test of Anglophone Solidarity

Joyce Ashuntantang & Dibussi Tande
Their Champagne Party Will End! Poems in Honor of Bate Besong

Emmanuel Achu
Disturbing the Peace

Rosemary Ekosso
The House of Falling Women

Peterkins Manyong
God the Politician

George Ngwane
The Power in the Writer: Collected Essays on Culture, Democracy & Development in Africa

John Percival
The 1961 Cameroon Plebiscite: Choice or Betrayal

Albert Azeyeh
Réussite scolaire, faillite sociale : généalogie mentale de la crise de l'Afrique noire francophone

Aloysius Ajab Amin & Jean-Luc Dubois
Croissance et développement au Cameroun :
d'une croissance équilibrée à un développement équitable

Carlson Anyangwe
Imperialistic Politics in Cameroun:
Resistance & the Inception of the Restoration of the Statehood of Southern Cameroons
Betrayal of Too Trusting a People: The UN, the UK and the Trust Territory of the Southen Cameroons

Bill F. Ndi
K'Cracy, Trees in the Storm and Other Poems
Map: Musings On Ars Poetica
Thomas Lurting: The Fighting Sailor Turn'd Peaceable / Le marin combattant devenu paisible

**Kathryn Toure, Therese Mungah
Shalo Tchombe & Thierry Karsenti**
ICT and Changing Mindsets in Education

Charles Alobwed'Epie
The Day God Blinked

G. D. Nyamndi
Babi Yar Symphony
Whether losing, Whether winning
Tussles: Collected Plays
Dogs in the Sun

Samuel Ebelle Kingue
Si Dieu était tout un chacun de nous ?

Ignasio Malizani Jimu
Urban Appropriation and Transformation: bicycle, taxi and handcart operators in Mzuzu, Malawi

Justice Nyo' Wakai
Under the Broken Scale of Justice: The Law and My Times

John Eyong Mengot
A Pact of Ages

Ignasio Malizani Jimu
Urban Appropriation and Transformation: Bicycle Taxi and Handcart Operators

Joyce B. Ashuntantang
Landscaping and Coloniality: The Dissemination of Cameroon Anglophone Literature

Jude Fokwang
Mediating Legitimacy: Chieftaincy and Democratisation in Two African Chiefdoms

Michael A. Yanou
Dispossession and Access to Land in South Africa: an African Perspevctive

Tikum Mbah Azonga
Cup Man and Other Stories
The Wooden Bicycle and Other Stories

John Nkemngong Nkengasong
Letters to Marions (And the Coming Generations)

Amady Aly Dieng
Les étudiants africains et la littérature négro-africaine d'expression française

Tah Asongwed
Born to Rule: Autobiography of a life President

Frida Menkan Mbunda
Shadows From The Abyss

Bongasu Tanla Kishani
A Basket of Kola Nuts

Fo Angwafo III S.A.N of Mankon
Royalty and Politics: The Story of My Life
Basil Diki
The Lord of Anomy

Churchill Ewumbue-Monono
Youth and Nation-Building in Cameroon: A Study of National Youth Day Messages and Leadership Discourse (1949-2009)

Emmanuel N. Chia, Joseph C. Suh & Alexandre Ndeffo Tene
Perspectives on Translation and Interpretation in Cameroon

Linus T. Asong
The Crown of Thorns
No Way to Die
A Legend of the Dead: Sequel of *The Crown of Thorns*
The Akroma File
Salvation Colony: Sequel to *No Way to Die*

Vivian Sihshu Yenika
Imitation Whiteman

Beatrice Fri Bime
Someplace, Somewhere
Mystique: A Collection of Lake Myths

Shadrach A. Ambanasom
Son of the Native Soil
The Cameroonian Novel of English Expression: An Introduction

Tangie Nsoh Fonchingong and Gemandze John Bobuin
Cameroon: The Stakes and Challenges of Governance and Development

Tatah Mentan
Democratizing or Reconfiguring Predatory Autocracy? Myths and Realities in Africa Today

Roselyne M. Jua & Bate Besong
To the Budding Creative Writer: A Handbook

Albert Mukong
Prisoner without a Crime: Disciplining Dissent in Ahidjo's Cameroon

Mbuh Tennu Mbuh
In the Shadow of my Country

Bernard Nsokika Fonlon
Genuine Intellectuals: Academic and Social Responsibilities of Universities in Africa

Contents

The Genuine Intellectual ix
Prolegomena xiii
The Credo xxiii
Preface to the First Edition xxv

Chapter One
   The University: Birth and Growth 1

Chapter Two
   Conservation and Reorganisation 15

Chapter Three
   Nature of Studies 29

Chapter Four
   The Scientific Method 43

Chapter Five
   Approach to History and Literature 59

Chapter Six
   Philosophy: A Categorical Imperative 71

Chapter Seven
   The Genuine Intellectual 85

Chapter Eight
   Dedication To The Common Weal 101

Chapter Nine
   Tributes to Professor Dr. Bernard Fonlon
   (19th November 1924 – 26th August 1986) 123

Books and Articles by Bernard Fonlon 141
Books and Articles on Fonlon 143

Portrait of Dr Bernard Nsokika Fonlon

The Genuine Intellectual

To Dr. Bernard Fonlon

A happy couple of humble background gave him life.
In remotest Nso he passed infancy unnoticed noticing.
The mirror of culture sealed an image in his memory,
And made Fonlon a child of the people, an object of hope.

The Whiteman saw in him a man, a bridge hard to damage.
He pictured mankind's harmonious co-existence with day dream success.
He dreamt heaven gate free with joyous expectancy;
And made Fonlon a staff of his mission, an object of hope.

With relentless zeal he explored the Whiteman's realm to knowledge.
He drained the wells within and looked without to Nigeria.
Miraculously he traversed evil infested rivers and forests
And in Enugu in Fonlon: hope disappointed, hope retained.

He forced the National University of Ireland to revise her academic records.
He won a place of honour in the Classical Oxford of England.
In France, he enkindled a literary fire that flames at the Sorbonne,
And Fonlon remained: and investment by mankind an object of hope.

Back in Cameroon motherly arms unfolded in triumph.
The people recognised him and asked for a helping hand.
He headed many a ministry and administered justice,
And Fonlon was: the pride of the nation, an object of hope.

He sowed the seeds of knowledge in the University of Yaounde.
With cultural, religious, philosophical and political writings he inspired creativity.

ABBIA Cameroon Cultural Review he founded and directs,
And Fonlon passed for a force to reckon with, an embodiment of hope.

While he lives, he listens to the voices wailing in the wilderness.
Let us seize and cage our double opportunity.
Let us read him and hear him and see him,
For Fonlon remains: A GENUINE INTELLECTUAL, an object of hope.

By Francis B. Nyamnjoh
18 June 1982

To Every African Freshman and Woman

Genuine Intellectuals: Academic and Social Responsibilities of Universities in Africa

Prolegomena

This book, slim as it looks, took me the best part of five laborious years to write 1965-9 inclusive. I was penning away as students in France were up in arms against the academic Establishment, and their fury almost toppled a powerful, prestigious, political giant like General de Gaulle (1890-1970). In America students, arms in hand, besieged and stormed the buildings of the University Administration, others blew up lecture halls in Canada - the student revolt, a very **saeva indignatio**, was in paroxysm. But in England (save in the London School of Economics where students rioted for the lame reason that the College gate looked like that of a jail-house) all was calm.

In France and America the students had good reason for the rising: the absence of Dialogue between student and Faculty, caused in France by the predominance of the Professorial System, caused in America by the involvement of the Faculty in Big Business research and the consequent neglect of the students. But old England thanks to a blending of the Professorial and the Tutorial systems, thanks to the wedlock of College and Faculty, thanks to the permanent dialogue that this blending maintained between the students and the University hierarchy, thanks to the share that students had in University government, thanks to this that even the newest freshman had the privilege of a hearing, thanks also to this that the University, by Charter, is independent of Westminster, England remained unruffled by the student insurgence.

Throughout that period, I was an academic on secondment to government and held successively the Cameroon Deputy Ministry of Foreign Affairs, the Ministry of Transport, Post and Telecommunications, and that of Public Health and Social Welfare – a humanist among technologists. And, in the running of these Ministries, I endeavoured to prove that even Politics and Government can be scientific and philosophical, that administration is best when it is subject to reason and principle and not when it is based on scheming and expediency. The deference with which I was treated by the highest specialists and the deep and lasting friendship I won from the best among them, proves, that I was right, by and large.

The question that readers of this book would ask, is whether the ideas I propounded ten years ago, on University Studies, on the organization of the Univer-sity, on the characteristics of the sterling intellectual, the genuine University man, have remained firm and unchanged, in my mind.

I make simple answer: From an analysis of the causes of the global student insurrection of the second half of the nineteen sixties, from my experiment with intellectual Government, from my experiences since I returned to the seemingly pleasing groves of academe - I am becoming daily more entrenched in my position, namely, in my views on the Nature of University Studies (Chapter Three), in the overwhelming importance of what Newman called 'influence and organization' in the establishment and running of the University (Chapter One), in my conviction about the genuine intellectual (Chapter Seven), in the need to remove all non-academic interference in University Affairs, in the need for enlarging scientific dimensions into philosophic horizons in University Studies (Chapters Four to Six), in this that if the University does not teach a student to think, it has taught him nothing of genuine worth, has failed wide of its mark, and lastly, in this, which I know will be hotly contested by many, namely, that the University is not for a mindless mob but for the Talented Tenth.

Such is my idea of what the University should be. And for it to attain these ends, for it to impart this manifold wisdom to the rising youth, for it to avoid prostituting itself, certain conditions are categorically imperative with regard to the choice .of teachers, with regard to the quality of students, with regard to University organization. This is fully discussed in Chapter Two.

Genuine Intellectuals: Academic and Social Responsibilities of Universities in Africa

Contents

The Genuine Intellectual ix
Prolegomena xiii
The Credo xxiii
Preface to the First Edition xxv

Chapter One
  The University: Birth and Growth 1

Chapter Two
  Conservation and Reorganisation 15

Chapter Three
  Nature of Studies 29

Chapter Four
  The Scientific Method 43

Chapter Five
  Approach to History and Literature 59

Chapter Six
  Philosophy: A Categorical Imperative 71

Chapter Seven
  The Genuine Intellectual 85

Chapter Eight
  Dedication To The Common Weal 101

Chapter Nine
  Tributes to Professor Dr. Bernard Fonlon
  (19th November 1924 – 26th August 1986) 123

Books and Articles by Bernard Fonlon 141
Books and Articles on Fonlon 143

Furthermore, any student seriously committed to intellectual enterprise must begin, even in his under-graduate days, to create the embryo of a library of his own, for he needs not only standard text books but also books of extended reading; and what better guide can he have for this than his chosen field and allied disciplines and others farther afield in which he develops an interest for general culture; and where else should he find these books than in a University Bookshop? As there will be other books above what his little budget can afford, or books out of print, or ancient and rare manuscripts, the University Library, well-stocked, well-run, becomes an absolute necessity.

This Trinity of Library, Bookshop and Press should be seen, at a glance, as a categorical imperative. But, is it not true that in some countries in Africa universities have come to being through a political fiat for glossy prestige and not through academic initiative to satisfy a genuine thirst for Learning; that the running of universities in the final analysis, is in the hands of persons who are anything you please, but certainly not seasoned academics? Is it not true that some universities are so fiddled with political meddling that they have become all but political outfits or worse? Is it not true that in this mess some highly qualified academics prostitute themselves to the point where they have lost intellectual integrity and have become base scheming politicians, Machiayellis in the Academy? How can intellectual enterprise blossom and bloom in such circumstances? Is it any wonder then that a good number of university men are not interested in scholarship, that in certain universities in Africa an alarming number of students distinguish themselves by a signal lack of interest in books, that some hardly read anything beyond their confused notes?

The degree or the diploma for earning a keep, in a remarkable number of cases, has become an end in itself, has become the *Summum bonum;* while the student dedicated to Learning for Learning's sake is held up to scorn as a queer.

If the book, as Carlyle preached, does not regain its primacy, if students are not brought up to become dedicated searchers after scholarship, then, whatever be the imposing number of universities that rise up in Africa, -only those, who will not see, will not see that we are heading for a society riddled with mediocrity and ineptitude (see more of Chapter Eight).

I had the good fortune, as a student, to see the inside of, and have a close look at, Oxford and the Sorbonne. To obtain a place in Oxford it took me two years of mighty work, writing to every Master of every College in Oxford and Cambridge, before I was finally admitted into St. Peters Hall, Oxford.

When I went to enrol myself in the Faculty of Arts in the Sorbonne, it took me by surprise that my case was treated not by prestigious Masters but by Secretaries. The young girls asked to see my degrees; thanks to the decision of *girls* I was now a member of the *Faculté des Lettres* of the ancient prestigious Sorbonne. The difference was remarkable.

Thereafter I became one of a nameless, faceless body of students. We trooped from one lecture hall to another but, outside of these there was no chance of establishing contact with any member of the Faculty. I was in my thirties at the time and proud of my independent spirit. Yet, I felt lost and lonely in this big Sorbonne. None of the Professors made any impact on me.

In Oxford, it was another story – completely. In St. Peters Hall we were under the Faculty care of a deeply religious Master, an Anglican clergyman, the Rev. Thornton-Dewsbury, who got up (it was whispered) every morning at five and went to the Chapel to pray for the students under his care. We ate together, after grace was said in Latin. Each one had a College tutor whom he had to meet at regular intervals to discuss their problems with him. The Undergraduates lived in the Hall under Spartan conditions.

In France, I saw the *Cités Universitaires* at Boulevard Jourdain and Antony from the inside. You rented a room there and came and went as you pleased; there were *Intendants*, but who had nothing approaching the authority and influence and the awe-inspiring presence of an Oxford College Master of the salutary contact and concern of a Faculty or College tutor.

A *Cité Universitaire* with its *Intendants* of no academic standing and prestige, no official or personal commitment to the welfare of the students, may be good enough for post-graduate students, but I would seriously doubt its efficiency in the intellectual, moral and social development of freshmen in particular, and undergraduates at large.

If you want my opinion, here it is straight and clear: I am for a system where undergraduates live under a seasoned fatherly Master, where, discipline is fostered and enforced. where salutary pride for the House is furthered, where the spirit of community life and responsibility is instilled, where the sexes live in separate halls.

I am not for a *cité universitaire* where individualism is rife and rank, where there is no authority to influence and inspire, where there is no discipline, and where promiscuity unfettered, unbridled, may turn the place, in the end, in spite of all its gloss, into a whorehouse.

Men, who pass through this institution that has withstood the trial and received the sanction of the ages, become genuine intellectuals equipped with a scientific and a philosophical turn of mind, concerned about the lot of man, full to overflowing with the milk of human kindness, strung up that, insofar as. the True, the Good and the Sublime are concerned, the dimensions and the horizons of their knowledge shall grow wider still and wider. Yet in spite of this, they shall be ever conscious of their weaknesses and their intellectual limitations as frail human beings contrasted with the puissance and the unlimited almost infinite vastness of Knowledge; and thus shall distinguish themselves by an uncommon degree of tolerance, meekness and humility (see Chapter Seven).

Now, let us take a look at a University next door, here in Africa, in Nigeria – Ibadan University, founded at five o'clock in the evening on the Second of February 1948, exactly thirty years ago. For those unfamiliar with the British system, it might be instructive to know that Ibadan did not begin with fanfare, as a full-fledged University but, very humbly as a University College under the careful superintendence of the University of London, and with able and efficient guidance of its first Principal, Dr Kenneth Mellanby; and did not become an independent University till ten years after and more, when, Nigeria became independent. Notice this also that in creating Ibadan, London University took for a model the Oxon-Cantab System.

Institutions wax and wane, and burgeon and bloom, and wither and decay, and die. And Ibadan is only thirty years old. Yet well begun is half done. But if Ibadan has remained faithful to the spirit of its founders, one can say, without fear of erring, that Ibadan ought to be, far and away the most prestigious University in Africa, and should be able to stand the test of time. Still its scholars and scientists are legion already, and, among them, are men of intellect and integrity, men with cultivated hearts, men with a sense of duty and a sense of public service, a sense of self sacrifice, a love of humanity so deep, so keen, so unswerving that they can be the envy and pride of any country, anywhere in the world; men who, in spite of the fact that their erudition and scholarship and achievements have spread their name around the globe, have remained, notwithstanding, for their sterling humility and self-effacement.

We have a shining example among us, the vene-rated (though I know he will protest with vehemence against the word) the venerable Professor Victor Anomah Ngu, M.B.,B.S., F.R.C.S. (London): F.R.C.S. (Edinburgh), M.S. Queen's Surgeon, Professor of Surgery Ibadan, a colonel of the Nigerian Army, Lasker Prize Winner for Cancer Research and pre-sently, Vice-Chancellor, University of Yaounde. The Nigerian Government, unknown to him were about to make him Vice-Chancellor of Ibadan University in 1971. I was at the time the Cameroon Minister for Public Health and Social Welfare charged, *inter alia,* with the formation of medical and paramedical personnel; the Cameroon medical School was barely three years old. And I needed him very urgently. I wrote pleading with him to come back home. 'Baring death I am coming,' wrote Professor Ngu. And he did. He came home to less alluring circum-stances, from every point of view, to those he had, without any illusions, abandoned, in

Nigeria. Any person who has had the chance to know him at close quarters will testify with me that his love for this country is completely unalloyed. He is a patriot to the core. And no one will say that Ibadan had no hand in making him what he is.

Another example is that of the now world re-nowned novelist, Chinua Achebe, whom I know, not out of books, but as a personal friend. His name figures among those of the first students, the 1948 batch. According to the text I have in front of me, Achebe graduated in 1953 with a B.A. General along with the Cameroonians, Peter Efange and the late lamented Eric Dikoko Quan, Minister Plenipoten-tiary in the Cameroon Diplomatic Service, when he died.

Achebe brought out his first novel, the classic *Things Fall Apart* exactly ten years after the opening of the University. That Achebe today is the foremost African novelist, whose works have become Classics in his own life time (he is still in his forties) is proof of the solidity of even a General Degree in the Ibadan of his day.

It is worthy to note that the Scholars who have put Nigeria on the map for high intellectualism do not come from among those who went to Oxford, Cambridge, London or Harvard; they come from Ibadan, by and large.

My eulogy of Ibadan is a eulogy by an outsider. And perhaps more convincing would be the matter-of-fact account of an authority who was one of the earliest Principals (1953-6).* And I will content myself with citing the passages which ram down the thesis I defend in this book on the Nature, End and Purpose of University Studies.

Since space will not permit me to quote extensively, this summary would suffice to show the account of an active eye-witness on how one of Africa's best Universities took birth and grew.

---

* J.T. Saunders, M.A., G.M.B., D.GL. *University College Ibadan*, C.U.P. 1960. I acquired the book years after writing my essay.

First, at least in the early years, conditions for entry were very stringent; for the authorities aimed at using the cream of Nigeria's rising Intellect to give the institution a solid foundation; and in this they went so far as to establish standards higher than those in Britain. The harvest of thirty years has proved them amply right, has vindicated the policy of selectivism in University admissions.

Second, they provided a teaching corps of the best minds consecrated to intellectual enterprise. Ibadan owes a deal to the calibre and dedication of men like Dr Kenneth Mellanby, the first Principal, Dr Christophersen, the Dane and (curious thing in Colonial times) the first Professor of English, Dr Saunders, Dr Onwuka Dike, and other distinguished academics.

Third, in order to instil discipline, good morals, salutary pride, healthy teacher-student contact and comradeship, the founders instituted the College or Hall-of-Residence system after the Oxon-Cantab model with men and women apart.

Fourth, and this is worthy of note, although Ibadan was a completely lay institution, religion as a solid and powerful bulwark in the moulding of youth, was fostered by the building of Chapels and a mosque right within the Campus-grounds and chaplains, university churchmen themselves, were full members of the academic staff.

In the fifth place, by the establishment of a free student government through an independent Students Union, these students were trained for future intel-lectual, active participation in public affairs.

And sixthly, all this was carried out under the vigilant trusteeship of the London University.

When I survey the rise and growth of this noble institution, the University, from ancient days to our time, I pay homage to Alexander the Great, to the Church and the Monasteries of the Dark Ages, to Carolus Magnus, alias Charlemagne or Charles the Great; but insofar as the University of our time is concerned, I salute John Bull.

Cameroon being a bilingual country, officially, the University of Cameroon is, *ipso facto,* a bilingual University, officially. And here homage must be paid to the State, to the University Authorities and to the students for the efforts they have made, in their various capacities, to make Cameroon stand out, as a State apart, in Africa, thanks to its official bilingualism in French and English.

But the question can, and should, be legitimately asked whether a policy adopted sixteen years ago still holds entirely good today. Are there no facts that have since come to light to bring us to contemplate a change or a substantial modification of this policy?

It is our duty to watch the world with scrutiny in order to see, not only situations that have arrived, but also those in the offing, those whose time has not yet come; to collect facts and data, to examine them intensively, extensively, coldly, dispassionately, and with intellectual honesty; it is our duty to scrutinize them with our minds shorn of foregone conclusions, to analyse them without mindless mirth or needless bitterness, and draw from them the conclusions that follow with syllogistic rigour.

If, in this particular case, we see that Science, Technology and Research are the levers that lift the world of today, and that we cannot effectively master Science and Technology without mastering the language of Science and Technology; if English is this language so absolutely necessary; and, if we conclude, as a logical consequence, that the progress of no country should be sacrificed or jeopardised to save another country's face, and that English must, therefore, become the first foreign language of this country, within the Academy, without the Academy; then we must say so, and say so without pleasure, and say so without rancour, and say so without wincing, and say so without gloating, and say so without mincing, and say so remorselessly, and say so unhesitatingly, and say so unrepentantly – and say so categorically.

The Credo

I believe in John Henry Cardinal Newman, Fellow of Oriel and Trinity, Oxford, Founder and first Rector of the Catholic University, Dublin.

I believe with him that the University should be an ideal land, a central Metropolis of Learning, where the True, the Good and the Sublime should be found in substantial-being.

I believe with Newman, that in the University, there should be no sovereignty but that of mind, no nobility but that of genius.

I believe that in the academy, rule should belong to Professors, and that, therein, princes should do homage.

I believe that for Professors to merit this homage, for them to ward off the prince's interference in acade-mics, their learning should be solid, their disinterested-ness, towards non-intellectual power, beyond all shade of doubt, their humility genuine, their heart over-flowing with the milk and honey of human kindness, their integrity unquestionable, their firmness in the right unshakable, their word and pledge absolutely inviolate, their sincerity transparent.

I believe that it is Professors imbued with these qualities that can exert, with efficiency, that influence which is indispensable for the *esse* of the University, and can set up, with effectiveness, and run, with skill, that organization absolutely necessary for the *bene esse* of the University.

I firmly believe and profess that thinking, even for its own sake, is the final end of Academic Enterprise.

I believe that while provisions should be made for each rising citizen to develop whatever skill or talent, with which he is blest by birth, through the establish-ment of specialized schools, the University, con-secrated to scientific and philosophical studies, should be reserved for those who are capable of scientific and philosophical studies.

I believe in God, as the fount and origin, the final end, the Alpha and the Omega, of all Truth and Goodness and Sublimeness, I believe that no right-minded makers of

Universities should ignore (not to speak of spurn) that Science which strives to make man's knowledge of Him more profound; they would be omitting the vitalest link, in the chain of College Knowledge.

I believe, therefore as Newman did, that the thought of God and nothing short of it, is the happiness of man.

I believe that it is by holding firmly, fervently, unswervingly, to this corpus of essential principles, I believe that it is by inculcating them scientifically and philosophically that the University can instil genuine, sterling, steep, unalloyed Wisdom, in whatever place, in whatever period, it lives and moves, and has its being, in the total *orbis terrarum*.

**Yaounde,
19 November 1977**

Preface to the First Edition

Fifteen years ago, back in 1954, I began my university studies in Ireland, in the city of Cork where

The Bells of Shandon
Sound so grand on
The pleasant, waters
Of the river Lee.*

As I look back, now, and memory brings to light the bright faces of the friendly youths and the charming colleens among whom I found myself then, I begin to wonder whether those youngsters, in their teen-agedness, had a keen, clear, and precise awareness of what they had come there for, of the sort of mind that university studies were meant to shape in them.

As it would have been anywhere else, I met there some very highly intelligent boys and girls; but, as I see it, now, almost all of them, to a man, were bent, foremost, on getting a degree, as fast as possible, obtaining a job thereafter, somewhere, in Ireland, England, America, Canada or Australia, and making a career. But I do not think that they knew (or cared, for that matter) what was the genesis of this age-long institution on which their future so much depended, or that they had a precise concept of the real nature, end and purpose of higher studies; and, consequently, a clear idea of how they could set about to co-operate with the faculty to exploit their chances, methodically, fully, in order to get, for themselves, the right sort of university education – something more than just a skill to wield, to earn their keep in life.

---

* 'The Bells of Shandon by Francis O'Mahoney - nineteenth century Irish Priest-Poet; a native of the City of Cork.

When I set foot in University College Cork, I was thirty years, of age, and had expended the larger share of those thirty years (in fact twenty-four all told) at school, at books. Just before going to Ireland, I had spent six years in an abortive bid for the Catholic Priesthood; three of which I had employed in an intensive course in Philosophy; the other three in Theology – courses which, rightly dispensed and tackled and assimilated, can give the mind a turn and bent and discipline which few other studies are able to instil. The professors told us that Philosophy was an *Ancilla* (a handmaid) to Theology, and was meant to prepare us for a more thorough-going study and grasp of that subject.

But as to the relevance of Philosophy to the other disciplines and to the complex problems of life, in the world, they said not a word; and, I am inclined to the mind that, highly intelligent and highly educated as they were (indeed some of them have left an indelible imprint in my mind for their learning, scholarship and humaneness), they did not see that there was a burning need to inculcate into us that there is a philosophical approach to every human question.

Thus, during a long university career, which took me from the National University of Ireland to the Sorbonne, in Paris, and to Oxford, my idea of the nature of university studies was not as clear and as precise as it ought to have been, considering my previous training and background. My predominant obsession, during those years abroad, was with the fact that, back home, Cameroonians were agitating for the reunification of the French and British sectors of the country, divided, between the Allies, since the rule of the Kaiser's Reich was ousted; and I was Dent on getting, for myself, as good and as thorough a training as I could, in order to help in building the reunited country – if it came. My foremost concern and preoccupation, at that time, was, obviously, not with the psychological and historical genesis and growth of the University, nor with the intrinsic nature and end and purpose of university studies.

During the last five or six years, however, I have given deep thought to this problem; I have communed with profound authorities on the subject, such as the eminent, nineteenth-century English Churchman, the famous Cardinal Newman; I have read current literature on university problems, and on what is now going down as the University Revolution; and I have come to certain conclusions on the subject. It may be that, since my university days, things have changed for the better and the students of today have a clearer, keener and more precise awareness of what university education is all about.

Notwithstanding, I have decided to put the fruits of my meditation and research before *the* African Student, at the threshold of his university career. And I do this in the hope that he will take my conclusions for what they are worth.

Bernard Fonlon
Yaounde,
6 August 1969

Chapter One

The University: Birth and Growth

We of the African race cannot remind ourselves too often of what the Blackman has gone through and of the condition in which he finds himself today consequent on centuries of tribulation. He was despoiled of all he had, despoiled of his rights, despoiled of his mind, despoiled of the will to resist; he was degraded, reduced to the level of the beast; in the words of a celebrated Oratorium: 'He was despised and rejected of men, a man of sorrows and acquainted with grief.'[1]

Today he finds himself right at the bottom of the pit, at the lowest rung of human achievement; he is struggling to rise, in the words of the famous psalm, *de profundis* – out of the deepest depths. The whole purpose of all his striving is to wring back from a hostile and unrelenting foe that dignity of which he has been reft. To achieve this, more is required of him than from any other race: more thought, more work, more energy, more faith in himself.

In the affliction of slavery, the slave yearned and strove for freedom; under the yoke of colonial rule, the African fought for independence.

Independence seems to have been won; but, before long it is dawning upon us that what we have won is the shadow and not the reality of self-rule. For, from being the slaves of our former masters, we have only been promoted to the

---

[1]. The Messiah (Air) XXIII: by George Frederick Handel.

dubious dignity of a beggar at his gate. We depend on him too much for the barest needs of life, and beggars do not have the liberty to choose.

Indeed, when you consider the arrogance of Smith, Verwoerd and Salazar and the hesitant attitude of the 'Western Democracies' in the face of the principle of equal rights for the black peoples, when you consider the part that these 'Democracies' have played in the spate of coups that Africa has seen in recent years and the cynical joy they derive therefrom, you awake to the fact that imperialist and reactionary forces are launching an offensive, an onslaught, against the forces of progress in Africa, for a reconquest of the continent. Make no mistake about it: the danger is real and imminent, and if progressive forces are crushed, if reaction rides in triumph, if African independence collapses, we are in for a yoke worse than any we have known.

Africa must unite, mobilize, to stem the tide of resurgent imperialism and to consolidate our political independence. This can only be done by loosening the foreign stranglehold on our economies; we must develop and exploit our resources rationally.

But what can we do to achieve this? To achieve this we need two basic, fundamental, absolutely indispensable means, namely, Knowledge and Capital.

Of these, knowledge is of greater importance in the order of things; for we all know that what has given the Whiteman his overwhelming superiority in the world is science, and one of the greatest handicaps that barred the African's road to progress was ignorance.

Even in the political domain knowledge is of supreme importance; for, as Aristotle has stressed, good government is not the work of chance but of science and purpose.

It can be asserted, therefore, absolutely, that it is principally through knowledge, coupled with skill, that the

Blackman is going to win that dignity which is the end of all his striving. Yes, it has been rightly said that knowledge is Power.

Up to this, in our plans for natural development, great emphasis has been laid on the political and the economic; and rightly so. But it needs to be stressed, again and again, that after the setting up of our political institutions, the next thing that should absorb our attention (at the same time as our economic development) is the creation and the consolidation of our institutions of higher learning.

In this essay, I intend to speak about the most important of these – the University – with reference to African needs and aspirations; and before I speak of it, from this point of view, I would like to say something about what the University is, in itself.

The word University comes from two Latin words *uni* (dative of *unus*, meaning **One**) and *versus*, meaning **in the direction of**, *toward, into: uni-versus*, towards one, into one. It connotes a movement, a combination of many things into one, the outcome is a whole. As an adjective, the word *universus* was used to qualify anything which resulted from the putting together of many parts into one. This was commonest in the expression *universus mundus*, meaning the whole world. As time went on, the expression *universus mundus* was replaced in general usage by the neuter of the adjective – *universum*, the universe, that is, all things that exist considered as forming one, the whole creation.

The Latin suffix *itas* (genetive – *itatis*) signifies a state of being: *unitas*, the state of being one or united, unity. *Universitas*, therefore, originally meant the **state** of things united to form a whole. Later on, especially in the Middle Ages, the meaning was extended to include the whole itself considered as made of parts; and further still to any group or body of persons, a corporation. And thus it came about that, by the end of the twelfth century, any gathering of masters and students in the prominent cities of Europe like Paris, Rome, Oxford, formerly known as a **Studium Generale**, a school of universal learning, a place of learning for all, became increasingly known as *Universitas magistrorum et scholarium,* a gathering, a guild, a community, of masters and scholars. Finally, the rest of the phrase was dropped and the **Studium Generale** or the *Universitas magistrorum et scholarium,* became known, from thenceforth, simply as a *Universitas* – a University.

Historically, therefore, a University meant, the gathering or the assemblage of masters and students from all parts of the known world into one spot, into one city, for the purpose of imparting and imbibing knowledge.

From ancient times up to the rise of European nationalism, after the fourteenth century, this geographical element of the University was the chief characteristic of its universality, namely, that it was an assemblage of teachers and students from **all nations**, in the then known world, for the promotion of higher learning. After that date, the emphasis shifted from nations to learning itself and it became truer to say that Universities were gatherings, communities, where **all branches** of learning known at the time were dispensed and imbibed.

The University, like every human institution, has a twofold origin, a psychological, that is a human need, and a historical.

The Genesis of the University sprang from the insatiate human craving for ever increasing knowledge. The workings of this craving, the stirrings of this urge, in the creation of this institution, were more evident in the early stages of its history, when other institutions that later played an active part, like the State and the Church, had not decided to take the initiative, or to bear a hand, in its establishment; when the University had not become the highly organised institution that we know it today.

There is, therefore, latent in man a demand, a thirst, for higher learning; and, whenever a teacher arose, notable for his talents and his attainments, a **supply** came into being, and scholars flocked from all sides, to drink at the spring. Therefore, what Cardinal Newman[2] has termed **influence**, that is, the irresistible attraction of a teacher of talent, attainment and repute, on young men, deeply desirous to render their knowledge more profound, was the essential cause of the emergence of Universities, especially in the early ages.

If any place in the Western World can claim to be the very *fons et origo* of Universities, Athens is the city that can rightly make that claim; for she was precisely the home of the earliest and the greatest philosophers, the mother of Western civilization; and, from the times of the earliest sages, she was, in herself, a veritable University – students flocked to her from every nation for higher knowledge, and teachers went there, from all corners of the then known world, to put their learning at the students' disposal.

First in time came the Sophists, prominent among whom was Protagoras (485-410 B.C.). Plato, in one of his Dialogues, named after this philosopher, described what a stir his coming caused in Athens, among the youth, in the days when Socrates was young.

Socrates himself (according to Plato) tells the story in the following words.

Last night, a little before daybreak, Hippocrates son of Apollodorus, Phason's brother, knocked violently on my door with his stick, and when it was opened, came straight in in a great hurry and shouted out:

> 'Socrates, are you awake or asleep?' I recognized his voice and said: 'That will be Hippocrates. No bad news I hope? "Nothing but good" he replied. 'I'm glad to hear it' said I. 'What is it then, and what brings you here at such an hour? "Protagoras has arrived', he said,

---

2. John Henry Cardinal Newman: *University Sketches,*

taking his stand beside me, 'the day before yesterday. Have you only just found out?'

'Only last evening." As he said this he felt for the bed and sat by my feet, adding: 'Yes, yesterday evening, when I got back late from Oenoe. My slave Satyrus had run away from me. I meant to let you know that I was going after him, but something put it out of my head. When I got back and we had had dinner and were just going to bed, my brother mentioned to me that Protagoras had come. Late as it was, I nearly came to see you straight away, then I decided it was really too far into the night; but as soon as I had slept off my tiredness, I got up at once and came here as you see.'

I recognized his determination and the state of excite-ment he was in, and asked him: "What is your concern in this? Has Protagoras done you any harm?' 'Of course he has, Socrates' replied Hippocrates laughing. 'He keeps his wisdom to himself instead of sharing it with me.'

'Not at all' said I. 'If you pay him sufficient to persuade him, he will make you wise too.'

'If it were only a question of that!' he said despairingly, 'I shouldn't keep back any penny of my own money, or my friends' money either. But this is just the reason why I have come to you, to persuade you to speak to him on my behalf. For one thing I am too young, and for another I have never seen nor heard Protagoras. Last time he came to Athens I was still a child. But you know, Socrates, everyone is singing his praises and saying that he is the cleverest of speakers. Do let's pay him a visit at once, to make sure of finding him in. He's staying, so I'm told, with Callias son of Hipponicus. Come on.'[3]

---

3. Plato: *Protagoras and Meno* (translated by W.K.C. Guthrie, 1956) pp. 39-40 Penguin Classics.

Another eloquent example of the role of influence in stimulating the thirst for higher learning is the story of the two Ambassador-Philosophers, sent from Athens to Rome, during the time of the great Roman leader, Cato (234-149 B.C.). He, as Censor, eaten up by burning zeal to stamp out the luxury that was beginning to corrupt Rome, saw with dismay the enthusiasm that these philosophers had enkindled among the people, and artfully got them dispelled, lest the yearning for Philosophy and eloquence, rather than that for prowess in arms, should emasculate the youth of Rome. The story is told by Plutarch:

> Marcus Cato was grown old, when Carneades the Academic, and Diogenes the Stoic, came as deputies from Athens to Rome, praying for release from a penalty of five hundred talents laid on the Athenians, in a suit, to which the Oropians were plaintiffs and Sicyonians judges. All the most studious youth immediately waited on these philosophers, and frequently with admiration, heard them speak. But the gracefulness of Carneades's oratory, whose ability was really greatest, and his reputation equal to it, gathered large and favourable audiences, and ere long filled, like a wind, all the city with the sound of it. So that it soon began to be told that a Greek, famous even to admiration, winning and carrying all before him, had impressed so strange a love upon the young men, that quitting all their pleasures and pastimes, they ran mad, as it were after philosophy; which indeed much pleased the Romans in general; nor could they but with pleasure see the youth receive so welcomely the Greek literature, and frequent the company of learned men. But Cato, on the other side, seeing the passion for words flowing into the city, from the beginning took it ill, fearing lest the youth should be diverted that way, and so should prefer the glory of

speaking well before that of arms and doing well. And when the fame of the philosophers increased in the city, and Caius Acilius, a person of distinction, at his own request, became their interpreter to the senate at their first audience, Cato resolved, under some specious pretence, to have all philosophers cleared out of the city; and, coming into the senate, blamed the magistrates for letting these deputies stay so long a time without being despatched, though they were persons that could easily persuade the people to what they pleased; that therefore in all haste something should be determined about their petition, that so they might go home again to their own schools, and declaim to the Greek children, and leave the Roman youth to be obedient, as hitherto, to their own laws and governors.[4]

Next to the Sophists came Socrates himself (470-339 B.C.) and we know that his influence on young men was so great that, in the end, he was tried and condemned on the charge of misleading them and on a charge of impiety.

Plato (420- 348 B.C.), his disciple and one of the greatest philosophers of all time, followed in his wake, and not only elaborated the system of philosophy for which he is celebrated but also founded the *Academy*, his famous School, for propagating his ideas.

After him came his disciple Aristotle, the philoso-pher who has exerted the greatest single influence on European thought and culture **from his day to our own**. He too founded at the Lyceum, in Athens, the institute which has come down to us *as the Peripatetic School*, so called from this philosopher's habit of lecturing while walking around the grounds with his pupils.

---

4. *Plutarch's Lives,* Vol. 1, p. 537. Everyman's Library, 407.

Athens fostered learning not only through her philosophers but also through her other institutions; for she was not only the home of **Thought** but also the home of the **Beautiful**, the cradle of **Democracy**. She had her celebrated sculptures, paintings, temples; she had the famous theatre where the deathless plays of Sophocles, Euripides and Aeschylus were acted; she had her political institutions.

This aspect of the history of Athens and Greece illustrates the role of **influence**, that is, the action of personality, the intercourse of soul with soul, the inter-play of mind upon mind, in the genesis of universities.

But the influence of masters however talented, however learned, however reputed, was proved, by experience, to be inadequate; for these sages, more often than not, were destitute men without the means to develop the institutions they initiated and render their action more effective. The help and the protection of wealthy and powerful patrons or institutions, especially the State was found to be absolutely necessary for the growth of Universities.

The first such patron of culture and learning was Alexander the Great (356-323 B.C.).

Alexander, son of Philip of Macedon and heir to his throne, was also the pupil of Aristotle. And thanks to this philosopher, who was also one of the greatest political scientists and literary theorists that the world has produced, the young prince acquired two qualities which were to have far-reaching effects, namely, a genius for administration and organisation, on the one hand, and a love of learning, on the other. A mere youth of twenty, on his father's death, he took up arms for the conquest of the world, subjugated Egypt, where he founded the city that is named after him, overran the Middle East, and pushed onward to the banks of the Indus in India. His troops refusing to go further, he repaired to Babylon where he died, shortly after, from an attack of malaria. Thanks to this union of the genius for sovereignty with an energetic devotion to letters, Alexander did what hardly any other conqueror of antiquity ever did. Neither Hannibal (247-183 B.C.), nor Caesar (101-44 B.C.) with all his cultivation of mind, conquered to civilise. But Alexander, both by his political institutions and his patronage of Science, sowed the seeds of culture as he went along. He was not destined however, as we have seen, to carry on this work himself for long, but his successors after him had caught his spirit and carried on his enterprise. For when he died, his empire was shared between two of his generals: Asia Minor fell to Eumenes; and Egypt with its capital at Alexandria fell to Ptolemy.

It is Ptolemy who supplies us with the first great instance of the establishment of letters; for he and Eumenes may be considered as the first founders of public libraries. Under the Ptolemys, a great system was set on foot for collecting together into one, and handing down to posterity, the oracles of the world's wisdom. It is said that, in the reign of the second Ptolemy, the volumes housed in the Alexandrian Library amounted to 100,000; in due course they grew to 400,000 and finally to about 700,000 volumes, as volumes were then formed. After lasting for over a thousand years, this library was deliberately burnt by the Seracens when they took Alexandria.

A library, however, was only one of the two great conceptions brought into execution by the first Ptolemy for the promotion of learning. For, prompted by Demetrius of Phalerus, he carried through a plan for the formal endowment of literature and science and founded a seat of learning, which he called the **Museum**, and supplied it with ample revenues. This institution combined with the library to make Alexandria a veritable University City. Thanks to this twofold institution, Alexandria super-ceded Athens as the intellectual capital of the world; and masters and students, allured by these facilities, flocked there from all parts of the then known world; and, for hundreds of years after, in fact, right up to the days of the early Church, this city became the abode of distinguished men and the centre of profound studies in Grammar, Rhetoric, Poetry, Philosophy, Astronomy, Music, Medicine, and other arts and sciences.

The **Museum** of Alexandria made its greatest contributions in the field of Medicine and Mathema-tics; for Galen, the celebrated Physician flourished in it. As for Mathematics, of four great ancient names on whom modern science is founded, three came from Alexandria: Archimedes was from Syracuse; but Diophantus and Apollonius of Perga were products of the Museum; so was the celebrated Euclid whose system of Geometry is known, and loved or detested, by every school boy.

Some of the outstanding writers and doctors of the early Church came from the Museum; prominent among them were Clement of Alexandria, Origen, St. Athanasius and St. Gregory Thaumaturgus.

With the rise of Rome, as we all know, Greece, as a political power, had to yield to the new ruler of the world. But about the influence of Greece on Rome, Horace has a very famous passage in the first Epistle of his second book.

> *Graecia capta femm victorem cepit, et artes Intulit agresti Latio: sic horridus ille Defluxit numerus Sarturnius, et grave virus Munditiae pepulere. . .*
>
> Greece captured made her savage captor captive and brought her accomplishments into rustic Latium. Consequently, the wild Saturnian verse passed out of use and elegance expelled the noxious venus of satire...

The Romans, with all their military might, had the humility to recognise a cultural superior when they saw one; had the humility to sit at his feet to learn; and, as a result, Roman students flocked to Athens, and Greek thought and art and letters transformed the Roman civilization. Among the Romans who went to drink at the Athenian fount of learning were such eminent writers as Horace himself, Cicero, and the Emperor Marcus Aurelius.

This reverence of Greek culture, on the part of the Romans, never waned. For Pliny the younger (A.D. 61-113) years later, writing to one Maximus who had been appointed governor of Greece, admonished him in these terms:

> *Cogita te missum in provinciam Achaiam, illam veram et meram Graeciam, in qua primum humanitas, litterae, etiam fruges inventae esse creduntur, missum ad ordinadum statum liberarum civitatum, id est, ad homines maxims homines ad liberos maxime liberos, qui ius a natura datum virtute, mentis, amicitia, foedere denique et religione tenuerunt. Revere conditores deos et numina deorum, revere gloriam veterem et hanc ipsam senectutem, quae in homine venerabilis, in urbibus sacra. Sit apud te honor antiquitati, sit ingenitibus factis, sit fabulis quoque. Nihil ex cuiusquam dignitate, nihil ex libertate, nihil etiam ex iactatione decerpseris. Habe ante oculos hanc esse terram, quae nobis miserit iura, qua leges non victis, sed petentibus dederit, . .*

Consider that you have been sent into the province of Achaia, that true and original Greece in which first civilisation, literature, even agriculture are believed to have been discovered, sent to regulate the condition of free communities, that is, sent to men who are truly men, free men who are truly free, who have maintained their natural rights by valour, by glorious feats, by friendship, by a contract in fact sanctioned by religion. Venerate the gods that founded the cities and the divine powers, honour their ancient glory and their present declining years, which in the case of man command respect, in the case of cities awe. Pay respect to them in their antiquity, to the great deeds of their past, even to their legends. Diminish nothing from any man s dignity, liberty or even vanity. Bear in mind that this is the country which sent us our laws, that she did not give us enactments after conquering us, but on our own petition.[5]

It is no wonder then that the masters of the Roman Empire, in so far as education was concerned, sought to emulate the good example of the Ptolemys. Teaching and learning were made a department of government and schools were set up and professors endowed, just in the same way as soldiers were stationed or courts opened, in the principal cities of the Empire. In Rome itself the seat of Education was in the Capitol. Of schools planted throughout the Empire, the most considerable were the Gallic and the African of which the former had a very high repute: Massilia (now Marseilles) one of the oldest of the Greek colonies, was the most celebrated of the schools of Gaul for learning and for discipline; it was here that Agricola received his Education. The Roman schools differed from the Alexandrian Museum in that, for the most part, they were devoted to the education of the young – *adolescentuli* – and had no reference to the advancement of science; Agricola came to Marseilles, when a child – *parvalus*. Their curriculum consisted of the Trivium and Quadrivium, that is, the three lower and the four higher of the seven liberal arts comprising, on the one hand, Grammar, Rhetoric and Logic, and, on the other, the Mathematical Sciences – Arithmetic, Geometry, Astronomy, and Music. To these were added Greek, Philosophy, Roman Law, and later on, Medicine.

Such was the genesis and the early development of higher education, such were the beginnings of Universities in ancient times. Through the genius and the energy of individuals, through the mission of single cities, knowledge was spread around the basin of the Mediterranean. And,

---

5. C. Pliny, *Epistuterum VIII, 24*.

thanks to its intimate alliance with political power, embodied in Alexander, the Ptolemys and the Caesars, learning received the means both of its cultivation and its propagation.

Chapter Two

Conservation and Reorganisation

The history of the advance of higher Education, unfortunately, was not destined to be so smooth. For it suffered reverses at the hands of the northern hodes that laid the Roman Empire low – the Goth, the Hun, the Lombard. The progress of letters and science would have been halted for ever but for this that another power came to the rescue and sheltered the treasures of ancient intellect during the convulsions; and bridged the abyss, and linked the old world to the new. This new protector of learning was the Church.

The barbarian invaders came in waves and their work of devastation went on, with moments of respite, now and again, from about the third to the sixth century. They spread all over the Empire like flights of locusts, and did their best to destroy every fragment of the old civilization and every promise of revival; for they directed their fury against the ancient culture, against the institutions in which it was embodied. It had become the fashion and the luxury, not only for every city in the Empire, but also for every colony and municipium, every temple and praetorium, even private villas, to have their own collection of books; Rome alone counted twenty-nine public libraries. But in their savage ignorance the invaders destroyed them wherever they found them. Thus they appropriated to themselves the territory of the Empire but not its civilization. From Germany and the north eastern territories outside the sway of Rome, they swept into Gaul, Spain, Italy; they crossed over into Africa.

For some time, Alexandria was spared, and it seemed that its Museum would survive as a hope for the revival of learning. But a century later Alexandria was taken and its library burned by the Seracens, an invader whose fury was even fiercer than that of the western barbarians.

As I have said above, these savage hordes could have succeeded in wiping out learning, completely, from the face of Europe, were it not for one power that withstood and survived them – the Church. And the Church preserved learning, thanks to two things – her monasteries, and the conversion of the Irish.

The Germanic peoples, that laid the Roman Empire and civilization low, swept mainly southward. A branch of them, however, the Angles and the Saxons, turned westward and crossed the Channel into Britain, and settled in that part of the country that is now present-day England. Thereafter, this island received no more of the dreaded visitations.

But her sister island farther to the west, then Hibernia, now Ireland, was spared the fury of the barbarian invader. Ireland was converted to Christianity, thanks to the labours of St. Patrick, in the first half of the fifth century. It was a country with nothing of that urban organisation that characterised the Roman Empire. There were no cities in which to place its bishops. Thus it was that the seat of the primitive Irish See was a kind of clerical village, founded for that purpose, where dwelt together bishops and clergy, monks and nuns. Because of this community life, these clerical settlements became monasteries, and, thus, the early Irish Church developed a marked monastic character. And in these monasteries two main pursuits formed the exclusive ambition of its inmates – sanctity and learning. Thus the Ireland of that era became the seat of a flourishing Church abounding in Saints and Scholars.

Owing to the fact that, after the Anglo-Saxon invasion, Britannia was not visited by the scourge of another barbaric host, the Christian Church was able to take a new birth, thanks to the zeal of Pope-Gregory the Great, who, having seen some Angle slaves in the market of Rome, determined, as he put it himself, 'to make the Angles Angels'; and sent St. Augustine, the first Bishop of Canterbury, to carry out this task.

Thus, when the old world passed away, with its wealth and wisdom, these two isles of the North became the storehouse of the past and the birth place of the future; the Celt and the Anglo-Saxon became the preservers, the cultivators, the custodians, and the propagators of learning, sacred and secular. It was thence, that, when the surges of the barbarian invasions had subsided, learning returned to continental Europe.

But, in this work of civilization, the Celt preceded the Anglo-Saxon; for Britain itself was partly Christianised by Irishmen, notable among whom was St. Columba; the Apostle of the Picts and the Scots; many English Sees, notably that of Northumbria, were founded by them; and, for many years, the famous Abbeys of Lindisfarne and Malmesbury were peopled by Irish monks and their Anglo-Saxon disciples. Some of these Irish missionaries crossed over to the continent; prominent among these were St. Fridolin who evangelised in France and in the Rhineland, and the famous Columbanus, whose missionary labours carried him to France, Burgundy, Switzerland and Lombardy, where he died.

The schools in the Irish cloisters, at this time, were the most famous in the West. Strangers in search of learning flocked to Ireland, not only from neighbouring Britain, but from remote nations on the Continent.

The seventh and the eighth centuries saw an increased effort, on the part of the Anglo-Saxons, in this evangelising and civilising enterprise. English Benedictine monks pushed into Germany and founded monasteries on which they settled down, to sing their chants and copy old manuscripts; and, thus, to lay the slow but sure foundations of the new civilization. Most prominent among these English missionaries was the Devonshireman Winfrid, more known as St. Boniface, the Apostle of Germany.

Such was the providential part played by these Northern Islands in the preservation and the propagation of European civilization. In lay and sacred learning, this period of their history is adorned by such illustrious names as those of John Scotus Erigena, the Irish philosopher, and Bede the Venerable, the English saint and Doctor of the Church.

When Charlemagne arose on the Continent, this special mission of the Celt and the Anglo-Saxon came to an end. Yet they were not superseded, till they had formally handed over the tradition of learning to the schools of France. For it was Alcuin, the Anglo-Saxon, who, on the invitation of Charlemagne himself, became the first Rector of the **Studium Generale** that developed into the University of Paris. An Irishman, Clement, succeeded Alcuin, and, another John, founded the School of Pavia.

The contribution of Charlemagne to the spread of Christianity, to the revival of learning, in this dark age, was so vast and so far-reaching that some have not hesitated to call him the founder of modern European civilization. We would understand better what he did, by first knowing who he was.

When the conflagrations that wiped out the Roman Empire had subsided, several kingdoms rose up, phoenix like, from its ashes. Foremost among these was that which the Franks set up in what was Roman Gaul – modern France. At the beginning of the eighth century, this kingdom came under the powerful influence of Charles, Mayor of the Palace of the Prankish king, surnamed the Hammer, because of the repeated slaughter with which he beat the Arab invaders that were swarming over into France from Spain. In 751,

Pepin, his son, who had succeeded him as Mayor of the Palace, felt himself so strong that he seized the kingship itself. Charles the Great or Charlemagne (768-814) succeeded Pepin and proved himself the mightiest warrior of this warlike family.

He proved himself to be the greatest figure that Western Europe had seen since Julius Caesar; in the History of the world he is lined with Alexander and Napoleon. He carried war into all directions and before long had made himself master of Spain, Italy and Germany and penetrated into the heart of Hungary, and became the Lord of the Western World.

On Christmas day, in the year 800, at St. Peter's in Rome, Pope Leo III crowned him Emperor of the Holy Roman Empire.

Next to the extension of his empire, Charlemagne had two other ambitions: the spread of the Church, and the promotion of learning.

Charles was not a mere brutal soldier; he was an educated man, a political idealist whose absorbing purpose was to organise the City of God on earth according to the principles laid down in St. Augus-tine's book, *De Civitate Dei*. For the first time in history, the Church had found a political genius wholly devoted to the task of realising the ideals of the gospel, whose burning ambition was to gain the world for Christ. In fact, so extreme was this zeal, that Charles dragooned entire peoples into Catholicism, and compelled them, by force, to receive baptism. Never before, and certainly never since, has Catholicism been so identified with a political regime.

He had insight enough to realise that piety that is not informed by sound doctrine is shallow. Thus the education of the clergy was one of his foremost preoccupations; he could not but realise also that, in order to run his vast empire, he needed the help of educated men; and his responsibilities made him painfully aware of the degree of the intellectual barbarism of Prankish Gaul. Thus Charlemagne became the greatest patron of learning since Alexander and the Ptolemys.

In the first place, he turned his attention to the Episcopal seminaries: these had been institutions of the earliest times of Christianity, but had been in great measure, interrupted amid the dissolution of society, consequent upon the barbarian inroads.

To these he added the grammar and public schools, as preparatory both to the seminaries and to secular professions. Each cathedral and monastery had to have such a school.

But what claims our special attention here is Charlemagne's contribution to the promotion of higher learning. The first thing is that he sought out eminent scholars, from all over Europe, and invited them to settle and work in his realm. In England, one of St. Bede's pupils, Egbert, promoted to be Archbishop of York, had founded there a school which, at the time of Charlemagne's accession, was the intellectual centre of Europe. It was Egbert's pupil Alcuin, head of the school of York, and the greatest scholar of the time, whom Charlemagne, as we have seen, persuaded to come over and settle in Gaul. He invited others from Italy and Spain.

It was asserted that Charlemagne founded not only grammar or public schools, as already said, but also the higher *Studio Generalia,* especially the **Studium Generale** which later developed into the University of Paris; that he confined these greater schools to certain central and celebrated spots in his Empire, places like Paris, Pavia and Bologna; and that he intended them, not only for ecclesiastics but also for the nobility and their children, as well as for poor scholars; that is, for every rank, class and race. In this he was in line with the ancient promoters of learning whose efforts had given rise to the Athenian School in Greece, the Alexandrian School in Egypt; and to those of Rome and Constantinople, under the Roman Emperors.

Although it can be debated whether the higher schools of Charlemagne were Universities in the strict sense of the term, it is beyond question that he commenced the noble work; without doing everything which had to be done, he did many things, and opened the way for more; he laid down principles from which the University sprang and grew, in that he aimed at educating all classes, and undertook the teaching of all branches of learning.

But in the succeeding centuries, especially in the Middle Ages, and, most especially, in the thirteenth century, -when no patron of learning as powerful and as zealous as Charles the Great came forward, events proved that such benefactors were not absolutely indispensable, for the creation and the growth of Universities. Even when they existed, they could only supply external aid and a frame work for the **Studium Generale.** But the real growth of Universities depended fundamentally and absolutely on a force innate to themselves – what Cardinal Newman, as I said before, termed *influence*, namely, that force of attraction which teachers of talent and attainment exert in a milieu where the thirst of knowledge is at work.

It was this influence, the principle of supply and demand, the existence of teachers of genius, the intrinsic attraction of knowledge, that caused Universities like Paris, Pavia, Bologna, Padua, Ferrara, Pisa, Naples, Vienna, Louvain, Oxford and Cambridge to rise or grow, at the voice of the philosopher or the theologian.

To take a few examples.

Bologna is celebrated in history for its cultivation of legal science, and was, at least, one of the earliest, if not the very earliest, of European Universities. A certain Inerius or Ivarner opened a school of civil law there at the end of the eleventh century; in the following century canon law was added, and, early in the thirteenth, a school of grammar and literature and those of theology and medicine.

Paris affords us a very striking example of how a University grows, thanks to the influence it exerts. For its school, from the beginning of the twelfth century, counted among its professors a galaxy of the highest talent in the history of medieval learning – William of Champeaux, the celebrated Peter Abelard, who, with great *éclat* taught, there, humanities and the philosophy of Aristotle, Peter Lombard, Alberic of Rheims, Hugh of St. Victor, St. Albert the Great and St. Thomas Aquinas.

In the twelfth century, a certain Vacarius or Bacalareus came up from Bologna to Oxford and effected a revolution in the studies of the place, by the devotion he enkindled for the study of law, and by the rival zeal this aroused in the schools of the arts and of medicine.

At Cambridge, the intellectual movement, which had already begun was greatly stimulated by the arrival there of four French monks who had been sent thither by Jeoffred, or Goisfred the Abbot of Groyland, who, himself, had studied at Orleans in France. They were versed in sacred learning and in Philosophy and attracted large crowds to their lectures.

These examples are very sketchy but they serve to show that, thanks to the self-originating, independent character of the scientific movement, thanks to the attraction of genius, thanks to the force of the law of supply and demand, Universities continued their vigorous growth, in the Middle Ages, in spite of the absence of a patron, of the stature of Charlemagne.

Up to this period, the basic University studies were the Arts, and the Faculty of Arts constituted the staples, as it were, of the University; in fact, it *was* the University. By the arts then were meant the two sets of studies that I have mentioned before, that is, the **Trivium** and the **Quadrivium**, namely, Grammar, Rhetoric and Logic, on the one hand, and Arithmetic, Geometry, Astronomy and

Music on the other. These were inherited from the ancient world, and were the foundation of the system which was then in the course of formation. But the life of the medieval Universities lay in the new sciences for which a sound grounding in the traditional studies served as a very useful, even indispensable prerequisite. Among the new sciences were Theology, Metaphysics, Law, Medicine, History, Languages.

As time wore on, two factors arose and proved that, although the attraction of genius, and zeal for knowledge, could be sufficient, in themselves, for the *esse* or the being of a University, they were not sufficient for its *bene esse* or its well-being, which has been technically called its integrity.

These two factors were the increase in members and the multiplication of the sciences. They brought to light the importance of another principle very vital for the life and the success of the University, namely, organisation: organisation of the student body, organisation of the studies.

Hitherto, with regard to the former, that is, the organisation of the student body, there had been but one governor over the students, who were but few and mostly from the neighbourhood. Now with the increase in the student population, it became necessary to divide them up into groups, and this was done on the basis of the part of Europe from which they came; and each group was called a Nation, and was placed under a head, who bore the title of Procurator or Proctor. There was nothing new in this, for, back in ancient Athens, students had been grouped on the same basis into Attic, Oriental, Arab and Pontic.

Just as the metropolitan character of the University gave rise to Nations and their Proctors, in the same manner, its encyclopaedic profession produced the Faculties and their Deans. According to the institu-tions of Charlemagne, each school had its own teacher, who was called Rector or Master; in Paris, Chancellor; elsewhere Provost. Even at the early stages, when the curriculum comprised the **Trivium** and the **Quadrivium**, it was difficult to find teachers qualified to profess all these seven sciences. But they became only parts of a whole system of instruction, which demanded, in addition, a knowledge of philosophy, scholastic theology, civil and canon law, medicine, natural history and the Semitic languages; and no one person alone could be equal to such a vast undertaking. The Rector fell back from his position of teacher to that of governor; and the instruction was divided among a board of Doctors each of whom represented a special province in Science. This is the origin of Deans of Faculties; and in as much as they undertook among themselves one of those departments of academical duty, which the Rector or Chancellor had hitherto fulfilled, they naturally became his Council. In some places the Proctors of the nations were added to this Council.

Another institution which emerged about this time in the life of Universities was the conferring of degrees. At first, they were only testimonials that a resident was fit to take part in the public teaching of the place. It was only later on that degrees became honours or testimonials, to be enjoyed by persons who left the University and mixed in the world. In the beginning, the University conferred them for its own purposes, to its own subjects, for the sake of its own subjects. But the recognition of the University by the State and by other Universities enhanced the importance and the dignity of degrees. However, the formal words by which they were denoted still preserved the memory of their early connection with teaching. For the students on whom they were conferred were called *Magistri,* that is, of the Schools, or *Doctores* and in some places *Professores*.

It was during this period that the term **Studium Generale**, applied, up to this, to institutes of higher learning, faded away and gave way to the title of *Umivetsifos*

Magistrorum et Scholarium, or *Universitas* for short, that is the whole body of teachers and students associated together as a society or a corporate body.

According to Cardinal Newman, the **Studium Generale** acquired the name *Universitas* firstly because of membership and secondly because of the, nature of its studies; it was the assemblage of strangers – teachers and students – from all parts, all countries, into one place; it opened its gates wide to scholars of all classes; it had for its profession the teaching of universal knowledge, all branches of higher learning.

The first characteristic, the geographical universality of Universities, was very marked indeed, in the Middle Ages, and this was made far easier still by the religious and the linguistic unity of Western Europe at the time – the Roman Church held undisputed sway and Latin was the universal language of scholarship. For instance, of the galaxy of professors who made Paris famous, at the time of which I am talking, few were fellow countrymen: St. Albert the Great came from Germany, St. Thomas from Naples, Peter Lombard from Navara, Robert Pullus from Exeter in England. Sometimes students were not content to study in one place but went the round of Universities to study at the feet of the most celebrated masters, and to get the best instruction in every school. There was also much co-operation among the Universities in so far as professors were concerned; it is said that exchanges of professors between Oxford and Paris were very frequent. With regard to the nationalities of the students, even a University as remote from Europe as Oxford, at a time when travelling was so difficult and dangerous, could count among its students Scots, Welsh, Irish, French, Spaniards, Germans, Bohemians, Hungarians, Poles. Such was the geographical universality of Universities, thanks to the religious and the linguistic bond that bound Europe together.

But as centuries rolled round the, spirit of nationalism awoke and grew, rivalries among peoples waxed into endless warfare, national languages took over from Latin and the gulf grew wider; finally, the Reformation came and made an end of religious unity. Consequent on these developments the ecumenical greatness of the Universities declined, and they became, in the main, national institutions, with regard to their membership.

They could remain genuine Universities by reason of the second principle which, together with their former international character, conferred on them the notes of universality, namely, the fact that, in spite of having become national, they remained faithful to their mission to promote, develop and hand down knowledge in all the branches of higher learning known at the time.

Speaking of Athens as a seat of learning, Cardinal Newman has given us in a lyrical passage, clear and succinct, an idea of what a University is:

> 'If we would know' says he, 'what a University is, considered in its elementary idea, we must betake ourselves to the first and most celebrated home of European literature, and source of European civilization, to the bright and beautiful Athens – Athens, whose schools drew to her bosom, and then sent back again to the business of life, the youth of the Western World for a long thousand years. Seated on the verge of the Continent, the city seemed hardly suited for the duties of a central metropolis of knowledge; yet, what it lost in convenience of approach, it gained in its neighbourhood to the traditions of the mysterious East, and in the loveliness of the region in which it lay. Hither, then, as to a sort of ideal land, where all archetypes of the great and the fair were found in substantial being, and all departments of truth explored, and all diversities of

intellectual power exhibited, where taste and philosophy were majestically enthroned as in a royal court, where there, was no sovereignty but that of mind and no nobility but that of genius, where professors were rulers, and princes did homage; hither flocked continually from the very corners of the orbis terrarium, the many-tongued generation, just rising, or just risen into manhood, to gain wisdom.'[6]

The salient points of this passage need stressing and clenching.

Where all departments of truth are explored; where all diversities of intellectual power are exhibited; where there is no sovereignty but that of mind, no nobility but that of genius; where professors are rulers and rulers do homage; where the rising manhood flock, for wisdom, from all corners of the *orbis terrarium:* – such is the University.

It is not my intention here to go into the nature of the University as it exists in our day, nor into the merits and demerits of the various systems of university teaching and organisation existing in various countries, nor into the causes of the current convulsions and upheavals that are shaking the world's Universities today to their deep-most depths and calling into question the centuries old, the consecrated, almost sacred traditions and foundations on which the University has stood, up to this.

Of these, there shall be question later on – if time allows. For the moment I must turn my attention to a problem which, to my mind, is of the highest and the most primordial importance, namely, the **Nature**, the **End** and the **Purpose** of University studies.

---

6. John Henry Cardinal Newman: *University Sketches,* p. 17. Browne and Nolan Ltd., Dublin.

Chapter Three

Nature of Studies

University studies are called higher studies. But in what sense are they such? Is it in the sense that more is piled up, indiscriminately, on what was learnt before, like so many stones heaped up into an enormous mound? But a pile of stones, however high, does not constitute an edifice. It has neither form nor order.

Higher studies are higher in the sense in which a well-architectured house is superior to a massive heap of stones. They must have order, a well defined structure, a system. In fact, they should be compared to something higher still; for University studies well done should be imbued with a principle of life and growth; a good education should be animated by that spirit of enquiry, that thirst for learning, which urges' the scholar to keep on searching for more and adding of his intellectual stature, as long as he lives.

University studies are higher studies, therefore, in two senses: firstly, that they are greater in quantity and quality, and, secondly, that they are more perfect in their intrinsic organisation. That University studies should be superior in quantity and quality needs no delaying upon; it goes without the saying. But what is it that endows them with their second characteristic?

As I see it, for University studies to have organisation, system, form, they must possess two indispensable qualities; first, they must be scientific; secondly, they must be philosophical. Let us deal with the first of these: University studies, to deserve that name, must constitute a science.

What is science?

Today, the meaning of the term science has been much restricted. Now, more often than not, it signifies an organised body of facts, known by means of experiment, regarding some aspect of the physical world. When men talk of science, today, they have uppermost in their minds Physics, Chemistry, Biology, as opposed to the fine arts, Sculpture, Architecture, Painting, Music, Literature. However, the word science has a meaning that is older, wider and more philosophical.

The word science, as you may know already, comes from the Latin words *scire, sciens, scientia* – to know, knowing, knowledge. Science is knowledge, but a special type of knowledge. To give you an idea of what science is in this more ancient, wider and philosophical sense, I will make a distinction between two types of knowledge – empirical knowledge and scientific knowledge.

In ancient times, there were certain physicians, medical practitioners, called the *Empirici*, because they drew their rules of practice from experience only. They were given the name *Empirici*, to distinguish them from their more thorough-going counterparts who, on the contrary, drew their own rules from experiment, from more systematic investigation.

The *Empirici* have given to the English Language the word empirical, used to qualify things that are known by experience only, things that pertain to, or are derived from, more observation. In so far as medical practice is concerned, we still have *empirici* among us today, only we call them native doctors, herbalists. Some of them have been known to cure diseases that have beaten the skill of modern specia-lists.

A native doctor knows, from having seen it several times before, that a potion, prepared from a particular herb, will cure a particular disease. But, of the nature of the action of the potion on the malady he knows nothing. He has never been able to analyse the constitutive elements of the herb in question. Apart from the external manifestations of the disease, he knows nothing. With regard to its internal nature, he is completely ignorant. Is the ailment functional, is it organic? Is it the influence of his personality, the confidence he inspires in the patient, that works the cure? He does not know. All he knows is that, whenever he perceives these symptoms and administers this potion, the sufferer improves, more often than not.

His knowledge of the medicine he administers and of the disease it cures is therefore empirical. He knows what happens but does not know why.

But suppose an African student doctor, researching for his M.D., carried out an investigation into the healing herb of his less enlightened brother, and analysed it into its chemical elements; suppose He further carried out experiments and found out that the disease was not merely functional but organic, and discovered the microbes that caused the malady and how they affected the organ they attacked; and suppose he carried his experiments further and determined precisely which of the chemical constituents of the herb was death to the germs and health to the patient, then he would know both the nature of the disease and the precise reason why the former cured the latter. Thus he would know, not merely that a certain herb cured a certain disease, but also how it did so. In brief, he knows not only the phenomenon but also its cause.

Such is scientific knowledge: the knowledge of things through their causes.

Let us take another example. From the beginning of the existence of man on this earth, men saw the sun rising, everyday, in the east and setting in the west. And for ages and ages, everybody took this phenomenon as a reality. Then, in the sixteenth century, Nicholas Copernicus, the Polish astronomer, gave the world a jolt by demonstrating that what the world had hitherto believed to be reality was, in fact, a visual illusion; he demonstrated that, in fact, it was not the sun that rose and set. but the earth' that revolved, round itself, once every twenty-four hours, causing night and day, and the apparent journey of the sun from east to west. After Copernicus, came the Italian scientist, Galilei Galileo, who thanks to the first ever telescope, confirmed the thesis of Copernicus and thus gave to the world scientific knowledge of the phenomenon of night and day, of the rising and the setting of the sun. Before the advent of these scientists, man's knowledge of this spectacle was empirical, that is based on the mere testimony of the eyes.

When we dig to the bottom of things to discover the causes from which they spring, our knowledge of them ceases to be superficial, disorderly; it acquires system, it acquires organisation, in this that we know also the foundation on which they are built, the inmost source or root from which they rise.

Scientific knowledge, therefore, to sum up, is knowledge of thing and cause; it is an organised body of truth regarding some special aspect of external reality. In order to grasp this definition thoroughly, it would be necessary to have a clear idea of what we mean by a cause.

The principle of causality is one of the ultimate principles of existence. It lays down that everything that comes into being, every event, every effect, must have a cause; whatsoever that begins to be, and is, must have a cause. In the process of becoming, cause comes first followed by its effect; cause is the antecedent, effect the consequent. Cause and effect are bound together by a bond intrinsic, absolute, metaphysical, belonging to the very nature of things. But I have not yet answered the question: what is cause?

A cause has been aptly defined as: that which makes a thing to be what it is.

Let us take an African mask as such a thing. Obviously, the mask-maker has made it to be what it is; his mind conceived it; his hand executed it. Secondly, there is the intention or the purpose which drove the carver to make his mask: did he intend it to decorate a dancer or to be worn by a member of a secret cult bent on striking terror? It is the purpose of the mask-maker which determines whether the mask shall be pleasant to look at or frightful to behold. Thus you can see that the purpose for which a thing is made contributes, in an essential measure, to make that thing to be what it is. Thirdly, there is the material of which the mask is made: wood, ivory, brass. It goes without the saying that this material contributes absolutely in making the mask to be what it is; for, without this material, there would be no mask at all, in spite of carver and purpose; this material is the very substance of the mask. Fourthly, there is the shape that the material assumes, thanks to the carver's skill and purpose – a human face, the head of a bird or animal. Maker, purpose, matter and form (or, in more sophisticated language, cause, the final cause, the material cause, and the formal cause) – these are the agents which combine to make anything, whatsoever, to be what it is; they constitute what in metaphysics is known as the fourfold causality.

To clinch the point home, let us take another example – water. Ultimately it was created by God, proximately it is brought into being by the forces in nature endowed with the power to bring it about. It has for purpose to slake the thirst of man, to irrigate the earth, to foster life in the animate world. Furthermore, scientists have discovered that it is made of two elements, hydrogen and oxygen. Lastly, water assumes a number of forms: it flows in streams, it surges in seas, it glistens as dew, it bites as frost, it freezes into ice, it rises as vapour, vanishes into thin air, condenses into fog or mist, sails in clouds across e skies and falls as rain, hail or snow.

Each of these agents – the forces that create it, the purpose it serves, the elements of which it is made, the form it assumes in a set of given circumstances – contributes an essential part in making water to be what it is. They are, in order, as I have said already, its efficient cause, its final cause, its material cause and its formal cause.

When we look at these two examples again, we see that the maker and the purpose contribute to the being of the thing from without, whereas the matter and the form contribute to the essence of the thing from within; they are inherent in the thing. In other words these four causes fall into two classes: the efficient and the final are extrinsic causes; the material and the formal are intrinsic.

The purpose, therefore, of all scientific investigation is, principally, to dig down, as far as possible, beneath the surface of phenomena to discover their causes and the laws according to which these causes operate, in order to bring these things into being.

Scientific investigation, then, is based on the immutable principle that whatever comes into being must have a cause. But this principle alone is not solid enough as a foundation for science. A systematic investigation into the nature of water would lead to no results if this substance were formed by hydrogen and oxygen, at one time, and by a totally different set of elements, at another. The chemistry of water could never exist if its cause were uncertain, inconstant. And this is true for any other phenomenon, whatsoever, in the material universe. Science is therefore possible, thanks, not only to the Principle of Causality, but also to another principle of primordial importance, namely the Principle of the Uniformity of Nature, or better still, the Principle of the Uniformity of Causality.

This principle states that all relations of cause and effect are constant and uniform; or in other words: the same, cause will, .under the same circumstances, always produce the same effects; and reciprocally, effects of the same kind are always the result of the same cause.

This is so because the connexion between cause and effect is not a mere time sequence of antecedent and consequent; a *post hoc propter hoc;* the sequence of two things or happenings, one going before, and the other following after, without any intrinsic link between them. For, as we have seen, a cause is that which makes a thing to be what it is; in other words, the effect depends entirely on the cause for its being. We can find in the cause the reason for every characteristic that the effect possesses; and it is by the action of the cause that they are communicated to the effect.

It is further manifest that every agent acts according to its nature, and can act in no other way; its active powers are proportioned to its nature; they are, in fact, the connatural expression of that nature. Indeed, we only know the permanent nature through the manifestation of its active powers. The nature or essence – for nature is but another term for essence – is the principle which determines, the character of these powers. Moreover, unless an agent possesses self-determination or free will, it must act in a manner not merely in accordance with its nature, but absolutely prescribed by that nature.

It is evident, therefore, that the bond that binds effect to cause is not a contingent connexion; it is not conditional or accidental, nor is it of uncertain occurrence. It is a physically necessary bond, rendering the production of the effect by the cause constant and uniform, in the material universe. Such then is the principle of the Uniformity of Causality, the *fons et origo* of all physical science.

Science, therefore, we have seen, is the knowledge of things through their causes; an organised body of truth regarding some special object of thought. In this definition stress is to be laid, as I have insisted all along, on the word organised.

Furthermore, the complexity of the physical world is prodigious: the circumstances which affect the operation of natural causes are so multifarious, and their accurate determination surrounded by so many difficulties that the progress of human knowledge is slow, and its victories won only at the cost of prolonged toil, by dint of endless drudgery. For nature does not reveal her secrets readily. Her processes are hidden and full of mysteries. We see enough to recognise that we stand in the midst of an ordered cosmos, but what are, the laws of that cosmos, we do not know. Thus the head of this mysterious web can only be unravelled by a search that is diligent, thorough and, above all, systematic. Here the word on which emphasis is to be laid is systematic; for without system there can be no organised knowledge, no science. Thus we can see the utmost importance of method in all scientific investigation. What, therefore, is method?

Method has been defined as a systematic manner of carrying on the search for truth. However, two separate subjects are generally included when we talk of the Scientific Method: firstly, the different ways in which scientific knowledge can be attained and pre-sented to the mind, and, secondly, the general rules which should guide us in the arrangement of our arguments, our reasonings. The first is needful to the research worker and the second to the thinker and learner in a field where research has already been done.

There are two ways in which the mind can acquire scientific knowledge: on the one hand, it may attain it by knowing first the cause and then from it move to its effect; by passing from a law or principle to the fact exemplifying that law; from the nature or the essence to the property; or, on the other hand, it may know first the effect and then dig beneath it to find its cause, *alis verbis,* it may pass from the property to the nature, from particular events to universal laws. One of these ways it needs must be; for, it is the essence of science that we know not merely the fact but the reason for the fact. We view the fact as the expression of a law of nature, the effect of a cause. In order to possess knowledge of this kind, we must either have passed from antece-dent to the consequent, from cause to effect, from law to fact, from nature to property, or vice versa.

These two scientific methods of knowledge are known respectively as Synthesis and Analysis, the Progressive and the Regressive Method, or, more commonly still, Deduction and Induction.

An example of a science in which Synthesis or the Deductive method is used is Ethics, the science which deals with right and wrong in conscious human activity. In this science, from the immediate or self-evident principle that good must be done and evil shunned, we go on to determine what is good and what is evil in particular concrete circumstances and thus, step by step, elaborate legal systems are built.

Another more pertinent science in which Synthesis or Deduction is the native process of the mind is Mathematics: our faculties give us an insight into the nature and the relations of discrete quantity and of spatial extension and figure and, thus, the mind is able to establish principles – rules, tables, theorems – which it uses in solving particular problems not only in Mathematics proper, but in all the other sciences which involve quantity and measurement. A very striking example of the use of the deductive method in scientific research is that of the distinguished French astronomer, Jean Joseph Le Verrier, who discovered a new planet without scanning the skies with any astronomical instrument. He did it by calculation alone. From a study of the solar system, of the force of the movements of .the then known planets round the sun, he came to the conclusion that there must be another, or else the system could not hold together. He calculated the movement of this unknown planet and determined the point at which it would be at a definite moment on a certain day. And there, precisely at that moment on that night, the planet was sighted from an observatory. They called it Neptune.

There is a perfection in Synthesis which is lacking in Analysis or Induction. In the metaphysical order, or the order of being, the cause precedes the effect. Thus knowledge finds its ideal, when the mind grasps the truth of principles, and, from them, reasons to their result. In such reasoning, we trace the path of Nature; the logical process is in full harmony with the ontological, the conceptual order with the real.

But, more often than not, in human experience, it is the effect which is first known before its cause; knowledge almost invariably begins from the concrete particular; it is from singular objects perceived by sense, that we must discover universal laws; it is from effects that we pass to their causes. Thus human science depends inevitably more on Analysis, or Induction, than on Synthesis or Deduction.

Induction, as we have seen already, is the legitimate derivation of universal laws from individual cases, the passage of the mind from effect to cause. For this, it is necessary to observe and examine several instances of the case under study until we are satisfied that we are justified in asserting a universal law of nature which embraces, not merely the specimens we have observed, but every member of the same class. It may even happen that carefully tested observation of a single case is held sufficient to justify a universal conclusion.

But the question may be asked: when are we sure that we have reached such a conclusion?

It is when we are certain that we are giving the name cause to that which is in fact the reason for the effect. When we have discovered the precise quality in virtue of which the effect is produced, we can then say, with confidence, that given these circumstances, this quality, this cause, will always have this same effect.

We are sometimes able to understand further the nature of causal relation, that is, the reason why such an effect should follow such a cause. The cause of malaria, for instance, remained unknown for a long time because of its minuteness. But as soon as its origin was discovered in a special microbe, and the activity of that microbe in the body had been studied, the nature of the relation which united the malady and the germ was evident. When it was known what havoc this minute creature wrought among the blood-corpuscles, it immediately became evident how the illness followed from the cause.

There are vast numbers of cases in which we can see no reason why a particular effect should follow rather than some other, and in which therefore the causal relation cannot be recognised. This is especially noticeable in regard to physical constituents con-sidered as the cause of a resulting compound. For instance, there is no resemblance between hydrogen and oxygen on the one side, and water on the other; the properties of the effect bear no likeness to the properties of the cause. In cases like this, however, our experience assures us as to the **fact** of the relation. But why such a cause should produce such a result remains a mystery, completely hidden from us.

To sum up, induction becomes possible as soon as we see, in the individual instance or instances of the cause in question, that the effect is not due to some accidental circumstances, but that it belongs essentially to the type. And this is known either by rational insight into the nature of the connexion between cause and effect, or by rational recognition of the fact of the causal connexion.

As we have seen, when experiment has established from a sufficient number of instances the fact that water is composed of hydrogen and oxygen, this principle can then be asserted not only of the specimens examined but of all water as such, no matter whether it takes the form of ordinary water, sea water, invisible water vapour, cloud, rain, dew, mist, frost, hail, snow, ice, sweat or tears. Thus inductive inquiry enables us to establish **universal** propositions or principles.

A universal principle is one that can be affirmed of all objects of the same character, if all individuals belonging to the same class, having the same nature.

Thus the end of all inductive investigation is to arrive at and establish such universal principles, to discover a nature, a causal connexion that can be affirmed of every member of the class of things in question.

The process through which the mind rises from the level of individual concrete cases to that of a universal concept or principle is called **abstraction** (from the Latin verb *abstraho, abstraxi, abstraction:* to pull out, to draw out of or from). When observation establishes, for instance, that the dog is a carnivore, we, in affirming this characteristic, abstract it away from all other considerations relating to the dog; we dismiss everything else concerning it, its size, its shape, its colour; we forget individual dogs and consider only the dog as such in all places, at all times, and fix our mind on this one point alone, namely, that all dogs feed on flesh. Such is abstraction, the mental process whereby, thanks to inductive investigation or analysis, we arrive at universal scientific principles.

To sum up this chapter, it can be asserted that all human science depends fundamentally, logically and chronologically, on Analysis or Induction. For all knowledge, in the nature of things, and in order of time, begins from the concrete particular. Even a highly abstract and deductive science like Metaphysics or Ontology must originate from experience; for, as an ancient rhymer once put it,

>Physics from Metaphysics begs defence
>And Metaphysics calls for aid on Sense.

Indeed, although deductive reasoning starts from the statement of a general principle, experience, inductive inquiry (and in some cases, indeed, even experimental science) must precede and lead to the acquisition of that principle. For there is historicity in all existence, even in that of abstract science. Such then is Induction or Analysis, the essence of the Scientific Method.

However, for Analysis to arrive unerringly at universal scientific principles, it must follow sure processes; and principal among these are Observation, Classification, Experiment, Measurement, Hypothesis. These we will now proceed to consider in turn.

Chapter Four

The Scientific Method

The problem which poses itself at the start of any inductive inquiry is, how are we to obtain our data, and how we must apply to these data our knowledge of Logic, in order to pass from them to the general fundamental principles of science. In other words, any investigation into the secrets of Nature and into their laws stands in need of Methodology.

To facilitate the finding of a solution to this problem, let us divide the objects that the universe offers for our contemplation into two kinds, namely, the static forms of Nature, on the one hand, and her dynamic activities on the other; in other words, essences and then" operations. The study of the first class gives us such sciences as systematic Botany and Zoology or the Classificatory Sciences, as they are sometimes called; and a study of the second, the Sciences of physical law, chemistry, light, heat, electricity, magnetism and so forth.

As we have already seen, Nature guards her secrets jealously; the threads of her mysterious web are not unravelled except by dint of diligent search. That is why Observation is a primordial process in scientific investigation; and this more especially where the study of essences, or the static forms of Nature is concerned. In the case of the study of her dynamic activities, Observation alone will not do. Experiment is absolutely necessary; but of Experiment there will be question later on.

Observation can be defined as the application of the faculties of man to the accurate determination of natural phenomena.

Obviously, the faculties that the investigator uses immediately in Observation are his senses. But senses without mind cannot go far: it is the intelligence of man that is the real observer; the senses are but its instruments.

Furthermore, if we try to take in, indiscriminately, all at once, the data that each phenomenon presents to us, we will only get confused. The mind cannot fix its attention, at the same time, on the myriad aspects of reality that sense perception presents to it.

The first rule, therefore, which must be kept, inexorably, if Observation is to be effective is that it must be selective. The mind, in studying any phenomenon, must concentrate its attention on one aspect of that phenomenon to the exclusion of all others. But in order that attention should be concentrated and fixed in this way, the mind must set itself, in every process of Observation, to answer a specific question. In other words, for Observation, to proceed surely, it must be made in the light of some hypothesis. Hypothesis are so important in scientific investigation that we must devote more space and time to them later on in this chapter.

Furthermore, for effective and successful Observation, the observer must possess definite qualities of sense, mind and will; physical, intellectual and moral qualities, that is.

With regard to physical qualities, the sense or senses that he employs in observing must be sound and keen. Those, for example, who suffer from colour-blindness cannot undertake observations in which the discrimination of colours is in question. At this level, man's inventive powers, in order to render Observation unmeasurably more effective, have fashioned for him auxiliary instruments capable of registering facts which lie far beyond the ken of immediate sense-perception. This fact has proved to be of the utmost value to science; for it has enabled enquiry, in diverse domains, to unearth phenomena which, otherwise, would have remained for ever undiscovered. To this category of auxiliary instruments belong the microscope, the telescope, the microphone, Rontgen rays and so forth, and so forth.

In so far as intellectual qualities are concerned, effective Observation demands, above all, that the mind, obviously, should be sound and keen. It must be that type of mind which does not rest satisfied until it has dug to the root of things. In other words, it must be a mind possessed by the spirit of inquiry, a mind urged relentlessly along by a burning thirst for knowledge. Without such minds, there would be no science, no philosophy.

The chief moral requisite which Observation demands is impartiality, intellectual honesty. This condition is not one that is easy to fulfil; for hardly anyone comes to the task of Observation unbiased. It is not easy to find persons who can register with perfect fairness, facts both for and against their own peculiar views. Each investigator has opinions and beliefs of his own and desires to see them confirmed, so that he may not have to face the difficulty of seeking new solutions to problems he already regards as solved. Openness of mind and candour are of the utmost importance in scientific investigation; for it is the first duty of the observer to accept the truth whether it be welcome or unwelcome. He must register facts as he sees them, as they are, and .refrain, scrupulously, from reading into them what he wishes to see.

For the purpose of scientific inquiry, we have already distinguished the natural sciences into two groups: those that deal with essences or the static forms of Nature and those that deal with her dynamic activities; and we have said that to the first group belong such studies as systematic Botany and Zoology and that Observation is the first requisite in the process of investigating into them.

Now, when we are studying animals or plants or other essences with a view to establishing universal principles about them, the first thing we do, after determining their characteristics through Observation, is to find out into what group they fall; in other words, we classify them. Indeed, Classification is so natural, so necessary, to these sciences that they are often referred to as the Classificatory Sciences.

The purpose of scientific Classification therefore, is to group individuals according to their species, and to group the species according to their natural coordination and subordination; for instance, the classification of animals as vertebrates and then as mammals, birds, reptiles, amphibians, fishes and then (according to their food) into herbivores, carnivores, omnivores.

The object which we propose to ourselves, in scientific or natural classification, is knowledge of the order which exists in Nature. In the natural grouping of the classes the mind perceives the unity, the harmony, the intelligence which pervades the whole creation.

From what goes before, therefore, we can see that the vast number of members, in the animal and in the vegetable kingdom, are, distributed into types and that these types possess not only certain broad resemblances but also a multitude of the most detailed characteristics common to every member of the class.

Furthermore, these similarities are not merely external; 'for they manifest themselves through the whole of the organism. Indeed, the complicated system of characteristics, of which the type consists, constitutes, in each case, a morphological unity, that is, a unity of form and structure. These characteristics unite to form a whole and each such whole is a closed system in itself.

Moreover, it is not merely the case that morphological structure is identical in all the members of the class, but, in addition, the processes of development, of metamorphosis, when it occurs, and of reproduction, are the same in each individual; and, as far as our experience reaches, are repeated, generation after generation, without change. Thus the type is endowed not only with morphological unity but also with biological unity.

The systematic ordering of the species according to their natural relationships is rendered possible by the fact that the numerous characteristics which constitute the type not only combine to confer, on the said type, a unity biological and morphological; it is also made possible by this that these characteristics have a hierarchical order among themselves, an order of subordination among their grades. For instance, investigators into the nature of the animal world have established that the characteristics of the mammal are more fundamental in the structure of an animal than those which belong to it as a ruminant; and those which mark it as a ruminant are more fundamental than those it possesses as a boss. The properties which distinguish the lower grades are subordinate to those which mark the higher. And the importance of a property depends on the position it holds among the characteristics considered in their natural subordination Those properties are most important which are fundamental in the structure of the animal, and which thus exercise a determining influence on the greatest number of characteristics.

The determination of properties and the setting up of a hierarchical order among them render possible and facilitate the framing of definitions; and it is when we arrive at accurate definitions that classification is attained. For when we have, by careful observation, worked out definitions, true and precise, classification is achieve; it is then we know, with a good degree of clarity, how Nature has distributed the real order into classes.

In so far as these natural classes are concerned, we must define by properties; our definitions, in this respect, are distinctive definitions; for, in them, both genus and differentia (that is, both that which the species has in common with the higher group and that by which it differs from other species in the said group) contain an indefinitely large series of notes; nor have we any means of knowing when we have exhausted the properties of any class.

To make Observation and Classification surer, Logicians advise the investigator to abide by the following rules in the process of his inquiry:

1. All groups should be so constituted as to differ from each other by a multitude of attributes.
2. The higher the group, the more important should be the notes by which it is constituted.
3. The classification should be graduated so that groups with most affinity should be nearest together, and so that the distance of any one group from the other should be an indication of the amount of their dissimilarity.

We have seen, firstly, that the purpose of inductive inquiry (and therefore of Observation and Classification) is to find out whether a causal relation exists between antecedent and consequent; we have seen, secondly, that to facilitate scientific investigation, it serves a useful purpose to divide the sciences into two groups, namely, those that deal with the static forms of Nature and those that deal with her dynamic activities; and we have seen, thirdly, that Observation and Classification are processes demanded, naturally, by the first group of sciences.

To render scientific inquiry more precise and surer, and knowledge profounder, a third process is necessary, namely, Experiment. This is all the more so in the study of the dynamic activities of Nature; for whereas the essences of Nature are relatively static, permanent and simple, her activities are transitory and occur under complex circumstances.

Observation, *as* we have already seen, is the applica-tion of the faculties of man to the accurate determination of natural phenomena.

Experiment differs from Observation in so far as, in Experiment, we observe the phenomenon under conditions which have been artificially simplified.

The necessity of this artificial simplification arises from the fact that conditions in which the said phenomenon *takes* place, as they occur in nature, are extremely complex. We should therefore be at a loss to distinguish which of the many antecedents was the true cause of the phenomenon, were it not possible to produce the said phenomenon in circumstances carefully determined, and thus to exclude the supposition that other causes were at work besides those we are engaged in considering.

A good example of such artificial simplification is afforded by the well-known 'guinea and feather' experiment, in which the two substances are placed in an exhausted receiver and allowed to fall from the top together. They reach the bottom of the receiver at the same moment, and, thus, demonstrate to us that when the resistance of the air and other interfering influences are allowed for, all bodies tend to the earth with equal rapidity. It is plain that without some method of simplifying the conditions, it would have been difficult, if not impossible, to obtain conclusive evidence of this truth.

I have said above that, before we set out to observe, we must set ourselves a definite and precise question to answer, a required-to-prove, as they say in Geometry. This is all the more so in Experiment. In other words, Experiment requires an hypothesis, necessarily. This means that, in the process of investigation, we must first, from our early groupings and experiments, frame some supposition and then set out to prove, by further experiments, whether this supposition is correct or not. Without this, no experiment is possible.

The mere use of scientific instruments does not in itself constitute an experiment. We do not speak of experimenting but of observing with a microscope. To make an experiment, it is not enough that the observer himself should be set in new and special circumstances. It is requisite that the object observed be placed under new conditions; and, further, that these new conditions should in some way modify its action.

In all cases in which Experiment is possible there can be no room for comparison between it and Observation; so complete is its superiority from the point of view of the scientific investigator. It is of limited value only where the activities of nature cannot be artificially reproduced; in such cases, we must be content to observe.

The advantages of Experiment over Observation are to be found in the fact that, by it, we are enabled:
1. to reproduce, under varying conditions, a number of instances of the phenomenon we desire to investigate;
2. to simplify the conditions;
3. to produce new phenomena of a similar kind.

With regard to the first advantage, it is hardly necessary to dwell on its importance. The science of electricity, for instance, would, very probably, never have emerged from infancy had it been possible to study it only during a thunderstorm. It is the possibility to produce electricity artificially under various circumstances that has enabled electrical science to make such giant strides.

With reference to the second advantage of Experiment over Observation, the ability to simplify the conditions under which the phenomenon is produced enables us to exclude any interfering circumstances and to control the phenomenon. Thus we are able to obtain certain knowledge instead of mere conjecture. Thus a scientist, wishing to prove that the trans-mission of sound is due to vibrations in the atmosphere, places a bell in a vacuum, rings it and no sound is heard.

The third advantage of Experiment is that it enables us to produce phenomena similar to those that nature presents to us. For example, from studying the evaporisation, the liquefaction and the freezing of water, scientists have been able to effect the liquefaction and the freezing of such substances as air, hydrogen and oxygen. Such experiments reveal to us facts analogous to those with which we are familiar, but which Nature uncontrolled affords us no opportunity of observing.

As we should be led to expect, having regard to the immense advantages possessed by experimental investigation, the sciences in which this has been possible are those in which the greatest progress has been made. Mechanics, Physics, Chemistry – all admit of experiment to a very large extent. In Anatomy, Physiology, Meteorology, it can hardly be employed to the same degree. It will not therefore surprise us that the former group of sciences has advanced far more rapidly than the latter.

We have seen that Experiment concerns itself more especially with the sciences which deal with the dynamic activities of Nature. By the very nature of things these sciences are concerned with motion and change. And where there is motion and change, however slight, quantity, space and time are essentially involved. And where there is quantity, space and time, weight, size, distance, speed come in automatically. And these are all entities whose amounts can be determined.

We can therefore see that Measurement is intrinsically connected with the sciences of physical law; for in them, as a matter of course, we are able to know not just what, but how much. Indeed, nearly all the stupendous discoveries of science have been the reward of long and patient labour in the minute sifting of numerical results; in other words, the result of precise and careful quantitative determination or measurement.

However, not all the laws of nature are capable of measurement. It is a perfect law of nature, for instance, that dogs are carnivorous; but this is only a habit, a quality which eludes measurement. On the contrary, the laws, for example, which govern the speed, the reflection and the refraction of light are capable of quantitative expression; those of Zoology, being purely qualitative, are not.

Yet it should be noted, however, that in those sciences in which Measurement is employed, the stage of accurate quantitative determination is always an advance on an earlier period in which investigation was concerned with quality alone. Naturally, we have to determine, first, what, before we determine how much. Thus, in Chemistry, the nature of the elements composing a compound is first discovered; the precise amount of each element is a subsequent stage.

To make what we say on this head clear, it will serve to have a look into the nature of Measurement.

All measurement is an act of comparison. To take the measure of a magnitude, is to determine the relation it bears to some other quantity, which we have adopted as a standard. As regards spatial measurement, for example, the standard measure-ment, for scientific purposes, is the metre and its sub-divisions. (The standard metre is a piece of metal preserved in Paris, which was originally intended to represent precisely one ten-millionth part of the earth's quandrant). For temporal measurement, the standard is the period constituted by the earth's revolution on its axis, namely, the day; this being subdivided into hours, minutes, seconds.

Measurement depends on sense-perception. But the senses are trustworthy only to a point and demand that their object should be proportioned to their powers. To ensure more perfect accuracy, and to render possible the measurement of things beyond the ken of the senses, instruments have been devised which enable scientists to determine quantities many thousand times finer than the finest sense can perceive. In some sciences, we are told, they are able to measure to the millionth part of a millimetre!

Indeed, the extent and the accuracy of Measurement of which modern science is capable must be accounted as one of its highest, one of its most useful achievements.

I have said twice before that, for Observation and Experiment to be sure and effective, Hypothesis is necessary. It is now time to say something more about the nature of Hypothesis.

It has been pointed out, again and again, that the purpose of all inductive inquiry is to find out whether a causal relation exists between a given antecedent and a given consequent. Let us say, for example, that an investigator is engaged in finding out the cause of a phenomenon D; thanks to his early observations and experiments, he notices that, more often than not, D is preceded by antecedents A, B and C. The question then arises which of these antecedents is the real cause of D. For one reason or other (its constancy for instance) the researcher, without being absolutely certain, develops a strong suspicion that the cause of D is C.

So he says to himself, 'Let me suppose that C is the cause of D'. A supposition of this kind is a hypothesis.

Having thus formulated his hypothesis, the investigator proceeds, by further observation and experiment, to find out whether his supposition is true or false. In other words, he endeavours to establish that the antecedent C always involves the particular consequent D and that D never occurs except when C has gone before it.

A good example is afforded by a series of experiments which were undertaken, in Uganda, to find out the origin of sleeping-sickness there. A series of careful observations were first made, and they appeared to establish that the disease was due to a certain microbe communicated to the blood by the bite of the tsetse fly.

The supposition was then made that the said microbe was the cause of sleeping-sickness.

On the basis of this hypothesis, further series of experiments were undertaken in which it was shown that, even where all the other conditions which usually accompany the disease were present, yet, if the germ was not communicated to the blood, the disease never appeared. Thus the causal relation between the germ and the malady was established and the hypothesis became a confirmed fact.

An hypothesis, therefore, is a supposition made with evidence recognised as insufficient, in order to account for some fact or law known to be real.

It is a provisional conjecture which accounts for known facts and serves as a starting point for further investigation by which it may be proved or disproved. In other words a hypothesis is a tentative explanation.

Discovery is almost entirely dependent on hypothesis. No man is likely to unearth a law buried beneath the complex phenomena of experience, unless he hazards an hypothesis, and then, by further observation and experiment, forces Nature to declare whether his hypothesis is correct or not. The first task of a scientific investigator, therefore, is to ask himself what various hypotheses, in themselves possible, may be imagined, which are capable of accounting for the phenomenon.

Yet, it must be emphasized that the posing of an hypothesis is only the beginning of the end; for notwithstanding the primordial importance of the role played by hypothesis in discovery, no part of the scientist's task is more important than the rigid test of suggested hypotheses. The aim of all investigation is the discovery of truth. To this, hypotheses are but means and instruments. The scientist must not become so captivated by the ingenuity of his hypothesis, and the accuracy with which it appears to explain the phenomenon, as to accept it as true, before he can say, with certainty, that the evidence is such as to exclude any other supposition. The greatest discoverers have insisted forcibly on this truth. Pasteur, for example, in his address to his colleagues at the inauguration of the Institut Pasteur had this to say:

> For the investigator it is the hardest ordeal which he can be asked to face, to believe that he has discovered a great scientific truth, to be possessed with a feverish desire to make it known, and yet to impose silence on himself for days, for weeks, sometimes for years, whilst seeking to destroy those very conclusions, and only permitting himself to declare his discovery when all the adverse hypotheses have been exhausted.[7]

Before bringing this head to a close, it will serve a useful end to say a word about how hypotheses are engendered. The origin of any hypothesis is to be found either in an induction based on grounds which are recognised as probable or in an analogy.

With regard to the first type of origin, I have shown that the process by which an inductive inquiry arrives at a scientific fact or law has two stages: a first in which Observation and Experiment lead us to guess that fact or law as probable, and a second stage where further assiduous and conclusive Observation and Experiment confirm the said fact or law. In this case the origin of the hypothesis is inductive.

Analogical hypotheses, on the other hand, as their name implies, are based on comparison: we observe that a new phenomenon acts in a way similar to some with which we are already familiar and whose laws we know; then we conclude that it is probable that the new phenomenon is governed by the same laws as the old. This may be illustrated by two examples in the history of Science, namely, the case of Sir Isaac Newton with regard to the moon and that which led James Watt to discover the steam engine.

---

7. Quoted in George Hayward Joyce's *Principles of Logic*, Chp. XXII, p. 353.

Sir Isaac knew that bodies near the surface of the earth are under the influence of gravity. He next observed that the moon resembles bodies near the surface of the earth. He then concluded that the moon **may be** under the influence of gravity.

James Watt once saw steam blow off the lid of a kettle. From experience he knew that ordinary agencies capable of raising weights do so by the exercise of motive power. In being able to raise the lid of the kettle, steam resembled these agencies. He therefore concluded that steam **may be** endowed with motive power.

In physical science, in addition to the term hypo-thesis, we often come across the terms Theory and Fact. Ordinarily, when a suggested explanation is held to have been satisfactorily proved and to be no longer open to question, it becomes Theory. A theory, therefore, is a hypothesis that has been confirmed or proved definitively.

The term Fact is sometimes restricted to mean any datum of experience, any real occurrence or phenomenon; sometimes it is extended to include whatever has been proved to be real; and, in this sense, the term Fact can be used of a theory whose truth has been established.

The process whereby, from the application of a universal knowledge of a universal whole, a universal nature, we arrive at the knowledge of a particular part or of an individual fact or thing; or, alternatively, and more usual and prevalent, the process whereby, through the examination and the study of individual cases – thanks to Observation, Classification, Experi-ment, Measurement, Hypothesis – we discover universal wholes, universal laws, universal principles, universal natures – these constitute Synthesis and Analysis, the Progressive and the Regressive, the Deductive and the Inductive methods of scientific inquiry and investigation.

It goes without the saying, as a matter of course, that these methods apply directly to the exact physical sciences properly so called. But, if the postulate or the contention that all University Studies should be scientific holds good, it remains to demonstrate how subjects, where exactitude, from the very nature of things, is not so rigorous, where the most we can hope for is moral certitude – subjects like History, Literature – can be scientific.

Chapter Five

Approach to History and Literature

The principal substance, the essential material, of which History is made is the corpus of events in the life of an outstanding individual, in the life of a community, in the life of a nation, in the life of the world, – events worthy of note, epoch-making events, as they are called, which determine the course of subsequent events and constitute landmarks, turning-points, in the onward march of that community, of that nation, or in the onward march of the world.

Getting the facts, all the facts, all the relevant significant facts, is the first and primordial duty of every historian.

If he was an eye-witness, in the thick of the things he recounts, so much the better. But even in this case, since he could not have been here, there and everywhere, all at once; since he could have been, not an impartial, detached, disinterested onlooker, but a committed partisan in the affairs, he would need the version of other witnesses to complete and correct his account.

More often than not, however, the recorders of history are not eye-witnesses themselves, and have to depend entirely on the testimony of others.

Just as objective, concrete, palpable evidence is the rock on which the exact .physical scenarios are built, just so, the testimony of witnesses is the foundation of all history. This testimony can be first-hand, or it can be obtained from those who learned the story from others; it can be oral; it can be documentary. Whether testimony is first-hand or second;

whether it is oral or written, one thing is absolutely essential the witnesses must be truthful in the fullest sense of the term, that is they must be objective and honest. Of this, however, there will be more to say later on.

But in getting his material from eye-witnesses or from documents, the Historian should take pains to consult as many versions as possible, in order to get the constant facts, in order to get to the core of things, in order to discard the irrelevant, to sift the wheat from the chaff and arrive at a version as complete as possible; because the omission of pertinent points can distort the whole story. In other words, History can be false not only when lies are told, but also when essential facts are left out. Significant events are, therefore, the material from which History is made.

But what it is that confers on History its especial character; in more philosophical parlance, what is the formal end of History?

That which makes History what it is is Truth; without Truth there can be no History; because

History is the faithful record of what really happened.

It is in this that History differs from the epic or the legend in which facts are enlarged and embellished to delight the popular ear and imagination. It is in this that it differs from the novel, which, although it draws its inspiration from facts, creates, nevertheless, characters, who, although they live intensely and love and hate and suffer and die in the book, never really existed as such outside of it. Of course, the tale and the fable are a farcry from History, being the almost complete concoction of a fertile imagination. In order to write objective, faithful History, in order to be a votary of Truth, a historian must possess certain qualities. If an eye-witness, he must be a keen and alert observer, with eyes and ears ever on the *qui vive;* if he is extracting the facts from documents, he must be a tireless drudger, probing every detail, discarding nothing. In either case, he must be a man of high moral qualities – intellectual honesty, the inflexible will to divest himself of preconceived ideas, of partisanship; else, he will produce incomplete truth or a twisted version of it. He must strive to give as complete a statement of the facts as possible; for a Historian can lie, as I have already pointed out, not only by blatant falsehood or telling half-truths, but also by the deliberate omission of relevant and essential facts.

This essential duty of telling the truth makes the writing of History a thankless and even dangerous enterprise, especially if the Historian has to reveal unpleasant facts about people in high places – alive and powerful!

Testimony, therefore, is the foundation of History; and for testimony there must be witnesses. These witnesses must have the same qualities as the historians - they must be well-informed, honest in mind; shorn of prejudice or bias; they must be people who have no vested interest in deforming the truth or hiding the facts.

When History is truthful, the hearers are **certain** of what they have been told. And **Certitude** is a very important state of mind, and an essential element, in so far as the attitude of man to science is concerned. Here, before going ahead, it would be useful to know what Certitude is; what kinds of Certitude there exist; and what degree of Certitude is conferred by History.

Certitude has been accurately defined by the Scholastic Philosophers, or the Schoolmen, as they are sometimes called, as – *'Firmus assensus mentis in verum sine formidine errandi'* – the firm assent of the mind to truth without the fear of erring. The opposite state of the mind to certitude and knowledge is ignorance which the same Schoolmen have defined as – *'Carentia scientiae debitae;'* the lack of truth that one ought to know. In between is the **doubt**, which is defined as the fluctuation of the mind between two contradictory or conflicting statements. There are degrees of certainty, which are determined by the degree of the firmness of the adhesion of the mind to truth, according to the nature of the evidence placed before it, in support of the assertion. In descending order, there is first Absolute or **Metaphysical Certitude** which is conferred on the mind by the very nature of being. I am metaphysically certain that a thing cannot be, and not be, at one and the same time; I am metaphysically certain that whatever comes into being has a cause. Obviously, the number of assertions for which this degree of certainty is possible is very, very limited indeed. The next degree of certitude is that which springs from the workings of physical laws. We are physically certain that the sun will rise at morn and set at sun-down; but has it always been so since the making of the world or will it ever be? We are certain that, thanks to the operation of geographical laws, rain will come at a certain time of the year; but sometimes, unexpectedly, it fails to come when it is due; at others, it fails to come at all! The laws of nature function with almost rigid regularity; they confer **Physical Certainty**; but they are apt to spring surprises. The lowest degree is **Moral Certitude**, which is conferred on the mind by the testimony of people that are well-informed, objective, unbiased, honest. Here we are on less firm ground; we are not governed by laws endowed with rigidity; we are in a domain where the chances of error are high; for our informer, though his sincerity be transparent, may be defective in ear and eye; he may be ignorant of other facts necessary for the establishment and the knowledge of the complete truth. Yet, where witnesses are clear-minded, well-informed, near to the facts; where they have no interest, however remote, in fraud or falsehood, the testimony of men convinces the mind and gives rise to genuine certitude. Moral Certitude on which History is founded, though fraught with danger of error, though less firm, is therefore, genuine certitude notwithstanding; else the science of History cannot exist.

We now come to the factors which create History, its efficient causes.

First of all, History is made by certain **Social Conditions**, some destructive, some constructive. Bitter antagonisms between classes, between nations, the clash of rival interests – these make revolutions and wars. On the other hand, the rise of burning needs, among men, has led to far-reaching events in the story of the world; the thirst for freedom, for instance, gave birth to Magna Carta, and subsequently to other revolutionary history-making legislation. History has also psychological causes. More often than not, men are surprised by events, caught in the storm and driven along irresistibly, against themselves. But now and again there have arisen, in the course of time, men, who, by their active genius, their unearthly personality, their force of character, their insight and foresight took the initiative and shaped the course of the story of the world – such were the great religious leaders like Buddha, Christ, Mohamed; such were the great philosophers like Socrates, Plato, Aristotle, and, modern times, Marx, Mahatma Gandhi; such were the great conquerors like Alexander the Great, Caesar, Charlemagne, Napoleon; such were evil, geniuses like Hitler and Mussolini.

Cultural causes play also an enormous part in making History. The teachings of the world's religious leaders aforenamed are an eloquent example. Such too have been the works of the great philosophers; such were the writing of political theorists, like Voltaire and Rousseau, Marx and Lenin, whose works set a ferment at work and lead to convulsions of world dimensions. It is true to assert that every revolution had its philosopher who went before it, and sometimes died without witnessing the explosions that his writings were destined to engender.

Finally, History has historical causes, History is made by other historical events. The revolutions, violent or otherwise, sudden or gradual, of which I have spoken above, are a clarion example. They change the course of the world, to such an extent that, after them, things are never the same again. In this class must be put also discoveries, such as that of the New World which gave birth to the great American nation and its Latin satellites, and to centuries of tribulation for the black man; man's landing on the moon, which will lead to we know not what! Such, too, are the great scientific inventions, such as that of the wireless, the aeroplane, the atom – things which have transformed the world out of all recognition.

Social antagonisms, national animosities, ambitions that run wild, extraordinary characters, historic upheavals, scientific inventions – these are the factors that shape the course of nations and the world – the efficient causes of history.

We now come to the reasons why history is taught and learnt or recounted. First of all, there is a natural thirst in any man born into .this world to know what happened before he came; that is why reciters of epics will always get an eager hearings Secondly, if an individual in a community feels that he has lived an outstanding life among his people, there arises in him the yearning for immortality, the yearning to live, after his death, in the stories told around the hearth, in recorded chronicles. Furthermore, each community is animated by the yearning to transmit to each succeeding generation the wealth of its past in exploits, in order to infuse into each rising generation, its particular spirit and character, and, thereby, mark it with the seal of its identity, and, thus, create for itself a historical continuum. At a more sophisticated level, historians seek to stimulate the young with the inspiration of great ideals, to set before them the example of great achievements, and cure dis-couragement with the consolation of great failures. For those who are destined to shoulder the burdens of the body politic, History serves a very useful purpose; it furnishes them with abundant lessons from the past, enables them to avoid errors and ward off, or forestall, communal catastrophes; it points out to them the road to follow, in order to foster the public weal. For, if they are mindful of their heavy and fearful responsibilities, it should be the ambition of public men to make history, to shape the course of events – not to be taken unawares, by these events, and driven along helplessly, like sheets before the wind.

I set out to answer how the study of a subject like History can become scientific.

The answer is now evident: .diligent research to get the facts about any happening; a scrupulous concern for the truth, by paying particular attention to the authenticity, or the genuineness, of the sources of information, to the veracity of witnesses, to the completeness of the account; a careful investigation into the social, cultural, psychological and historical causes of the event under study; the lessons men can learn therefrom, the contribution it can make to ward off disaster, to make a happier world these are the factors that raise ordinary story-telling up to the level of science.

History is a subject that embraces everything, that enters every field; individuals, communities, nations, the world, every invention, every subject of study – all have their history. It is a subject that cannot but clarify, foster, complete and enrich the study of all other subjects, a study that men neglect or despite to their cost.

Now, the question we are attempting to answer is, how the study of a subject like Literature can be scientific.

Literature, whether it be the lyric, the epic, the fable or tale, the short-story, the novel, the play, the essay, a philosophical treatise, is one expression of the beautiful; the other forms being Music, Painting, Sculpture, Architecture. Beauty is not conferred on a work by chance; it is the result of conscious, specific causes at work.

The study of a literary specimen becomes scientific when the student endeavours to discover, not only whether the said specimen is beautiful, but also why it is beautiful; to discover, that is, the material, the formal, the efficient and the final causes that create that beauty.

The substance of which Literature is made is the Life of man, either as it has really been lived (History), or as created by the ingenuity of a fertile imagination (fiction). Every element of human life can be the subject of Literature,

Thought, for example, being the highest human activity is, par excellence, material for Literature, especially when it is profound.

Feeling that is deep is another; and, thus, love and hate, joy and sorrow, fury and exhilaration, frustration and satisfaction, hope and fear, are material for Literature.

Such likewise is **Action**: heroic achievement, prowess in war, and even the humble annals of the lowly, can be fitting substance in the making of Letters.

Man does things, but he also suffers others; in His life there is **Action**, but there is also **Passion**, like that of Christ. Thus the misfortunes of the human kind can become in a very marked degree the very essence of Literature. Under this heading fall the heartrending conflicts which can sometimes rage within the human soul, or those that pit together powerful rival parties; such is the case of the clash of powerful principles, views, interests, prejudices; such are the tragedies and catastrophes that strike and overwhelm individuals, nations and the world. In a word, all that provokes awe or exhilaration, tears or laughter, is substance for Literature.

A scientific study of Literature, therefore, must begin with an examination of its content.

There are certain qualities that literary material must possess to be worthy of the name.

First of all, it must be true, or at least, (in the case of fiction) **be true to life**, as the saying is. It must possess that quality that is referred to in French as *la vraisemblance,* and which can be loosely translated, into English, as 'likelihood'; the reader must be under the impression that this did happen or could happen. The unlikely and the insincere vitaite Literary material.

Furthermore, literary material, within each **genre**, or literary form, must be developed to the full to its logical conclusion. Material that is defective, or arrives at the wrong conclusion, vitiates good writing.

Another quality of good literature is symmetry or proportion: there must be a clear pattern on which the work is based; the forces at war must be of matching strength; the various parts into which the work is divided must be proportionate to each other. Lopsidedness mars a work of art.

A study of the content, therefore, is the first duty in the scientific examination of any literary work.

But content alone, however over-awing, does not make Literature. To become this, it must be expressed in Language of exceptional, or at least, of more-than-normal beauty. Language is the form, or the formal cause, which contributes to make Literature what it is. Indeed, the role of language in this field is so primordial, so preponderant, that there is Literature that is such on the strength of the beauty alone of the Language in which it is expressed.

In this, I have an authority to bear me out, and, if I am not mistaken, it is Shakespeare himself.

> The poet's eye, in fine frenzy rolling,
> Doth glance from heaven to earth, from earth to heaven;
> And, as imagination bodies forth The forms of things unknown, the poet's pen Turns them to shapes, and gives to airy nothing A local habitation and a name.[8]

---

8. BREWER R.F., *Art of Versification*, p.

Yet, the first law in this question is that Language, the Form of Literature, should so fit the Matter as to become one with it, indistinguishable from it: the container should fit the content, the suit should suit the wearer. In Literature, the use of what the French call *le mot juste,* and the placing of each word just where it should be in the sentence, are of the utmost importance.

Laying down the law on exactness in the use of words, *aiiis, verbis,* on Simplicity in writing, Horace, the Roman poet, had this to say, in-his *Ars Poetica:*

> *Ex noto fictum carmen sequar, ut sibi quivis Speret idem, sudet multum frustraque laboret Ausus idem: tantum series juncturaque pallet, Tatum de media sumptis accedit honoris.*
> I will strive after language composed of well-known words, such that anyone might hope for himself to attain, but should sweat much and toil in vain when he attempted it: such is the power of order and context, so great the dignity that can be added to common words.[9]

Speaking of the force that words acquire by being put in their right places he said:

> *Ordinis haec virtus erit et venus, out ego fallor, Ut iam nunc dicat iam nunc debentia did. . .*
> The power and the beauty of arrangement, or I am much mistaken, will prove to lie in this, namely, to say at the very moment what at the very moment should be said. . .[10]

Language is composed of two essential elements, to wit, sense and sound; and each of these has its own share to contribute in making language beautiful.

With regard to sense, thoughts that are noble and profound, deeds of heroism, confer an intrinsic beauty on language.

---

9. HORACE, Ars Poetica, p. 132 v. 240-243
10. ibid. p. 126 v. 42-43

With regard to sound, words have music or melody, which they acquire from the vowels and consonants that compose them; when linked together in well-ordered phrases, clauses and sentences, they become endowed with rhythm.

Furthermore, the imagination of the writer en-hances the beauty of literature by the wealth of the imagery with which he enriches his writing.

In like manner, and subjectively, the imagination of the reader canhighten the beauty of Literature by the images, the associations and the memories that the reading of this Literature creates or calls forth.

A study of language, and all that goes with it, is the next step in the scientific investigation into the factors that endow a piece of writing with beauty.

Aristotle wrote: 'For a speech is composed of three things, the Speaker, the subject on which he speaks, and the audience he is addressing'.[11]

The matter and the audience in mind determine, to a very large measure, the nature of the language that the author will use. But in the very nature of things, any piece of writing, whatsoever, is influenced, to a very far-reaching degree, by the author himself: his intellectual ability, the fertility of his imagination, his temperament, his ease with words, his background and environment, his training, his loves, his hates.

There are certain types of literature, lyric poetry for instance, which are best written in the flush of youthful feeling. But more often than not, the great masterpieces of the world's literature have exacted more than that. Most of the great writers – epic poets, novelists, dramatists – because they wrote about human life, and human life is complex to the point of being complicated, spent years in observation

---

11. Rhetoric 1.3; quoted by Herbert J.C. Grierson in *Rhetoric and English Composition*, p. 15

and study and training and practice and endless drudgery, especially in the use of language; because art is not easy to acquire. In most cases, they were seasoned by this that they themselves went through thick and thin, knew storm and stress, and joys, and the harrowing sorrows of the soul.

In other words, scholarship and experience and unrelenting labour are necessary for the making of a *chef-d'oeuvre;* and the saying that genius is nine-tenths perspiration and one-tenth inspiration, is true, more often than not.

Therefore, a study of the life and times of an author deepens the understanding of his works and makes the readers' knowledge of them scientific.

Finally there must be an inquiry into why the writer wrote: was it to overawe or to delight and amuse? to draw tears or laughter? to charm? to stimulate elevated sentiment and purify morals? to instruct? or to inveigh against the evils of the day? This purpose determines, in large measure, the form of the piece of writing; and a study of it deepens and renders scientific an understanding of the work in question.

Such then are the factors that make the study of Literature scientific, the factors whereby we discover, not merely, that a literary work is beautiful, but, more especially, why it is beautiful.

Chapter Six

Philosophy: A Categorical Imperative

I set out to show that University Studies, if they are to be worthy of the name, must be scientific and philosophical. Thus far, I have striven to demonstrate how such studies can be rendered scientific. I now turn to the second part of this treatise, namely, that for University Studies to merit their dignity and prestige, they must also be philosophical. But to do this, there is no other approach more logical than to begin by saying, clearly, what I mean by philosophy. For here I am entering a field rank with division and debate.

Instead of giving a cut-and – dried, ready-made definition, I propose to lead the reader up to my idea of Philosophy through a classification of the main sciences – a classification based on the relative wideness of the portion of the universe covered by each of these.

In general, all the sciences deal with the physical universe. But each science differs from the rest according to the particular aspect of the universe that it treats.

A science which covers only the living world is narrower in scope than a science which covers both the living and the non-living world. A science which deals with only one species of the properties of the Universe is narrower in scope than a science which deals with a range of properties wider and related.

Furthermore, each science of narrower scope falls within the sphere of every other science of wider scope; each science of narrower scope has its roots in, and presupposes, the sciences of wider scope.

In our classification of the sciences, from the narrower to the wider, let us begin with Biology. Biology is the science which concerns itself with that portion of the universe that is endowed with life, or what is more commonly referred to as the living world, the world of living organisms.

Chemistry, on the other hand, is the science which deals with the composition of complex material substances from simpler physical elements; or, inverse-ly, with the decomposition of composite bodies into their diverse component elements. These building-up, these breaking-down, processes take place both in the animate and the inanimate world. It follows, therefore, evidently, that the field covered by Chemistry is wider than, and englobes, that covered by Biology. It follows, furthermore, that a prior and thorougher knowledge of Chemistry would give to the student a profounder knowledge of Biology; since, as I have said, Chemistry includes Biology and Biology presupposes Chemistry.

Next we come to Physics. Physics is the science which deals with Change and Motion in the material world; it concerns itself with that singular property of the physical universe without which no change or motion, whatsoever, is possible. This all important element, this indispensable property, is Energy. Physics deals with the various sources and the various manifestations of energy in the world. Heat is one. Light is another. Sound is one. Electricity is another, Magnetism is one. So also is Nuclear Energy.

In like manner, chemical composition or decomposition is but one manifestation of Energy at work in the world. Indeed, without some of the forms of Energy, like heat and electricity, for instance, no chemical composition or decomposition is possible. Even life itself is a manifestation of change and motion and energy in the universe. It follows logically then that the field of Physics is far wider than, and encircles, that of Chemistry and Biology.

It follows as logically that a prior and deeper study of Physics will render deeper still the mind's grasp of Chemistry and Biology; for it will lay bare the root and fundamental causes without which no Chemical or Biological process is possible.

The next science, with regard to extent of scope is Mathematics. Mathematics: concerns itself with all that has extension – extension in space, extension in .time; however infinitesimal, however enormous in magnitude, that extension may be. It deals with quantity, both when that quantity is in a state of motion, and when it is in a state or rest or inertia. It is the science of all that is capable of measurement – quantity, animate or inanimate, with all its properties like size, volume, weight, composition, activity; it concerns itself with energy in all its manifestations; with space; with speed.

Mathematics, of all the physical sciences, is that with the largest scope; within its ambit, or sphere, fall Physics, Chemistry, Biology. Indeed, no student needs to be reminded that Physics and Chemistry and certain sections of Biology so depend on Mathematics for exactness that, without it, they could not possibly exist as sciences, with precision as their foremost property.

Mathematics, therefore, the science of widest scope in the physical world, deals with quantity, which is the most inherent property of matter. When you say of matter that it is quantified, you have said the most fundamental thing that can be said about it.

At this point, the question arises whether beyond quantity, beyond matter, anything else exists. There is a phalanx of learned and prestigious philosophers: who say no. For my part, though without learning and prestige, I say yes. And saying so with me are the millions who believe in the existence of a non-material human soul, in the existence of a spirit world, in the existence of God. Besides the visible, sensible world, there exists another, beyond the reach and ken of eye, and ear, and smell, and touch, and taste.

The universe considered in its totality comprises the material and the non-material, the embodied and the unembodied world.

Is there any final, fundamental property which belongs to both, the last property of the total universe, that is found in anything, whatsoever, that exists?

The answer is yes. The answer is that everything that is, is;' in other words, whatever is, is endowed with Being.

Being, therefore, is the element which embraces the total universe; it is the final property of all existence.

Beyond Being, there is **Nothing**.

All the Sciences that we have seen can be considered as forming a series of concentric circles: the smallest of these circles delimits Biology, which deals with living organisms; the second is the sphere of Chemistry, which concerns itself with the elements, the composition and the decomposition of matter, whether living or non-living; the third circle is the scope of Physics, which is the science of the sources, the manifestations, the effects and the uses of energy; the fourth is Mathematics, which has for its object quantity which is the ultimate property of the material world. The outermost circle, englobing all, is the science which treats of Being, the property of the total universe.

This final and all-embracing science which treats of the nature, the forms and the properties of Being is Metaphysics, the science of the universe, the science of the universal.

It is Metaphysics that is Philosophy in the strictest sense of the term.

Philosophy, therefore, is the science of Being as Being, the science which treats of the principles and causes and qualities, inherent in all things, whatever they may be, merely from this alone that they are, that they exist. Since Being is the final, most universal property of things, it follows, consequently, that philosophy is the science which concerns itself with the final, ultimate, most universal, all-embracing, principles or causes of the total Universe.

I have defined Science succinctly as knowledge of **thing** and **cause**; Science looks for immediate, specific causes. Philosophy goes further: it searches for the ultimate, most universal causes of things. It is also a science; the difference between Science and Philosophy is not, therefore, one of **kind** but one of **degree**: for, if Science is the knowledge of Thing and Cause, Philosophy is the knowledge of **thing** and **ultimate cause**.

What are these principles or properties that flow from things *ipso facto*, or that belong to them merely from this alone that they are, that they exist?

First of all, whatever is must be what it is, must be itself and not something else. Artificial hair, for instance, may be so perfect as to deceive both sight and touch, but for all that perfection it is not real hair. This simple, obvious-looking, statement is the all-important metaphysical principles of Identity: everything that is must be what it is, else knowledge is impossible.

Secondly, there is the principle of Causality which, as I have said before, states that everything that comes into being must have a cause.

Thirdly, everything that is must have that which makes it what it is, must have an Essence, or, to use more ordinary language, a Nature.

Furthermore, everything that is must possess that by which it is, that by which it exists, that is, its *Existence*. Therefore, anything that exists really, in the concrete, here and now, must have an Essence or a Nature and an Existence; else, it cannot be, else it is not **something**, but **nothing**. Essence and Existence are the ultimate elements of which all things are composed.

Further still, everything that exists has the power of *Becoming*, either more of what it is, or of becoming something else; in other words, it can Change its nature; it can change its place, or increase or diminish its space. The weest baby born is already, potentially, a full-grown man; the stoutest, heftiest man, brimming with health and bursting with energy, is potentially, the dust we all become, after death, food is potentially living flesh; wood is potentially ashes. The process of Becoming involves two terms or stages; the stage at which the thing possesses only the power to become more of itself or, something else, and the stage at which it really or actually becomes that something else. These principles or stages or terms in the process of Becoming are known in philosophical jargon as Potency or Potentiality and Act.

If a thing is really what it is supposed to be, if it possesses its genuine essence or nature, we say that it is True.

If it has, to the full, all that it should have to be what it is, *aliis verbis,* if it has no defect, no excess, but the right measure of its being, we say that it is Good.

If being what it is, and fully so, it further pleases and delights eye or mind or both, by the fullness or completeness of its being, by the symmetry or proportion of its parts, by its splendour or colour or *éclat* or brilliance (which-ever you will) we say that it is Beautiful. Truth, Goodness and Beauty are some of the fundamental and intrinsic properties of Being. In other words, Being viewed as genuine, viewed as lacking nothing that is due, viewed as charming eye and mind, is variously and correspondingly referred to as the True, the Good and the Beautiful.

It is the study of these principles and properties and others more, into which we cannot go at present, (like the Unity, the Analogy, the Transcendence of Being) – it is this study that constitutes Metaphysics.

By long meditation on this subject, I have been won to the view that Metaphysics is Philosophy in the strict and absolute sense of the term.

The other branches of Philosophy are Philosophy, either by the application of metaphysical principles to particular and restricted fields, or by a comparison of those fields to Metaphysics. They are not Philosophy strictly and **absolutely**, but only **relatively**, in other words, by analogy.

For example, if in our study of the physical material universe, we push beyond such properties as life, as structure or composition, as activity or motion or change and the forces from which it springs, to find out what is the most universal, the most all-embracing property of matter, we come to the conclusion that everything material, be it solid, liquid, gas, has quantity, has parts beyond parts, is a continuum, has extension. Furthermore, we see that that which has extension, must also have place and duration, in other words, it must exist in Space and Time. In addition, everything that is quantified must have the Matter of which it is made and the Form in which it exists. Therefore, when, in our study of the physical world, we push our investigation into the ultimate principles and properties of that world by asking ourselves what is the nature of quantity, what is space? what is time? what is matter? what is form? what is motion? what is change? we find ourselves in that field of philosophical studies that some call Natural Philosophy, others Cosmology, others Ontology. These are questions that have worried thinkers from the days of Thales, the first philosopher, to our own.

In like manner, when in the study of such a well-defined, distinct and limited sphere, like the living world, we pass beyond such problems as the com-position of living organisms, their irritability to specific stimuli, reproduction, growth, decay and death, to ask ourselves, what is the origin and nature of life? what is the highest form of life? in other words, what is the labyrinthal nature of the soul of man? what is feeling? what is will? what is mind? – we are in that field of Philosophy that is called Psychology.

Likewise, when, in the study of the **conscious**, **rational** activities of man, we bend ourselves to find out, what is the ultimate end that all men, at all times, seek in all they do? what is the first, final and most fundamental law that should govern and guide them in this quest? what are the indispensable means he must use to achieve that end? in other words, an inquiry into the nature of genuine happiness, the *Summum Bonum* of man, an inquiry into the first, final, fundamental universal **norm of morality**, into the nature of **obligation** and **right**; – this is the field of philosophical studies generally referred to as Moral Philosophy or Ethics.

In each of our investigations into each of the domains mentioned above, we are doing one of two things: we are either applying the principles of Metaphysics to a particular, restricted, well-defined field, or we are digging for the universal, ultimate, fundamental, all embracing principles and properties that govern, or belong to, all things within that field. In each case, we are philosophising, not in the absolute sense, as in Metaphysics, but in a relative sense.

Yet my deep conviction is that the study of no philosophical discipline can be complete, coherent and profound without a study of Logic and Meta-physics. Logic prepares the mind for the inquiry; shows it how to proceed surely; gives rules of thought to go by; it is a propaedeutic and normative science; Metaphysics gives you an all-embracing view of the universe, divides Being into its categories, puts everything in its place.

Having defined Science and having said how university studies can be made scientific; having now defined Philosophy, I come to the second part of my two-fold question, namely, how university studies can be rendered philosophical.

Let me begin by stating the ideal. If life were not so short, if the period of it propitious to studies were not so brief, if there were not these myriad, complex subjects clamouring to be studied, in preparation for life, I would say that all university studies should be preceded by, or accompanied by, or followed by, a thorough course in Logic and Metaphysics especially, and (why not?) in all the other philosophical disciplines. There is hardly any other course of studies so calculated to put order into the mind: it would give the student, as I have said, an all-embracing view of the world; it would give each thing its value, by placing each category of being where it should be, in the entire universe, by putting each science in its place in the total system of human learning. Logic especially will give method, clarity and precision; obviate confusion and prevent the student from beating about the bush. Speaking for myself, in my long life at books, no course ever gave me so much satisfaction, I have never found any course so absorbing, so useful, so sobering as the three years (too short alas) that I spent in Philosophy.

This ideal, the study of all the lengthy, complicated philosophical disciplines, will not be possible in the vast majority of cases; indeed, some would reject such a proposal today as a surprising irrelevance! The next best thing is that the study of each science should be preceded by, or accompanied by, or followed by (which-ever you please) a study of the branch of philosophy on which the said science is based. A few examples will make this clear.

Law is the study of that body of rules, whether customary or formally enacted, which a state or community recognises as binding on its members or subjects for the preservation of public harmony and welfare and the promotion of individual good.

Politics is the science and art of government, the science which deals with the regulation of its relations with other States.

Social Science or Sociology is the study of the origin, the history, and the constitution of human society or parts thereof.

These are all sciences dealing with the conscious, rational, multiform activities of man as an individual, and, most especially, as a member of a group.

It goes without the saying that the study of the ultimate universal end towards which all these activities should tend, namely, the well-being or the **happiness** of man; the study of what true, genuine happiness consists; the study of the ultimate means without which this end cannot be achieved, to wit, **duty** and **right**; the study of the universal, ultimate norm of morality, of the nature of justice, of the nature of moral good and evil; – it goes without the saying that a thorough knowledge of the science which deals with all these, that is, Ethics or MoralPhilosophy, will deepen and consolidate and act as a firm foundation for the study of Law, Sociology and Political Science.

Another example is Medicine. Medicine is the science and art which concerns itself with the cure, the alleviation and prevention of disease; with the restoration and preservation of health. It is now almost universally recognised that such is the intimate union between body and soul, flesh and mind, that serious disturbances in mind can .lead to serious disturbances in the functioning of the body. Thus diligent inquiry into the genesis, the nature and the termination of life, into the nature of mind, will and emotion, into the maladies that can afflict them; in short, a study of Psychology, the science of the nature, the functions and the phenomena of the human mind and soul, will surely render the study of Medicine sounder and profounder; thus Psychoanalysis and Psychiatry are recognised, today, as essential companions of modern Medicine.

In like manner no study of Education can be complete without a thorough study of Child Psychology. One can almost assert, without fear of contradiction that, if Education and School Method neglect this indispensable study, they are almost sure to run off the rails.

Another example, is History. There is a popular that no event can happen twice; what has been, is past and gone, and gone forever. In the scientific study of History, as I have said before, we concentrate our attention on the assembly and the verification of all the relevant, necessary facts, on the examination of objective evidence, on the scrutiny of the veracity of witnesses, on the genuineness of testimony, on the causes remote or immediate that produced the event. But when we transcend the particular, individual irrepeatable historical phenomenon and its causes, and plunge into the human soul in the search for those forces, in man, which provoked the event, a revolution, let us say; *aliis verbis*, when we investigate into the psychological causes of the given event, we are looking for permanent, fundamental, general, universal forces which would drive man to react in like manner, at all times. Thus we give to the study of an individual phenomenon, limited in space and time, universal dimensions. It is this method that would render the study of History so useful and so indispensable to those charged to direct and shape the public affairs of men. Without this, narrations of historical events are as good as fairy tales, fit only to thrill the eager ears of children. History, philosophically studied, tells not merely what has been; but, more significantly, what is most likely to happen, if men embark in a certain course, if certain precautions are brushed aside. It is in this sense that I the saying that History repeats itself acquires meaning and justification.

In the scientific study of Literature, we are intent on finding out those qualities or properties, in material or content, in form and expression, in the author, in his purpose; which qualities or properties, confer beauty on a piece of writing. Now the Beautiful, as I have said already, is one of the expressions, or one of the Metaphysical properties of Being. Therefore, a study of the Beautiful and of its higher and most intensified form the Sublime; on inquiry into those properties or qualities in any form of Being that fill the mind with pleasure and admiration or sometimes with awe – completeness of development or fullness of being or grandeur; colour or *éclat* or brilliance or lustre (whichever you please); symmetry or proportion in the disposition of parts; the power or the force with which the *ensemble* strikes and over-powers the mind; – such a science is the very foundation of literary studies and cannot but render these studies sounder and profounder.

In like manner, an investigation into the nature of quantity, of matter and form, of motion and change, of space and place and time, cannot but serve to deepen and consolidate a study of Biology, Chemistry, Physics and Mathematics; for these properties of Being are the very bed-rock of the physical sciences.

Logic is another example. It is that branch of Philosophy which deals with the forms of thought in general and especially with inference, reasoning and the scientific method. As I have said already, it is a propaedeutic and normative science. It prepares the mind for scientific and philosophical studies by giving it the principles whereby it can inquire surely and acquire precisely, concepts; enables it to make accurate definitions, classifications, and judgments; and to reason with rigorous correctness. In brief, Logic directs the mind in the search for, and the acquisition of truth – Now, there are hardly any two things more naturally, more inextricably welded together, fused into one, indeed, as **thought** and **language**. It goes, therefore, without the saying that a firm grasp of Logic will render firmer and profounder a knowledge of language; and result in more precision in the use of words, and to greater rigour in the saying that History repeats itself. But it is obvious development of thought. A study of Logic, therefore, will immensely enhance, and render more penetrating, the study and the use of Language.

What I have said in the fore-going chapters, though brief and sketchy, will help to make clear, I hope, what I mean, when I say that University Studies should be scientific and philosophical, that is, that in their pursuit, the intention should be to lay bare, not only facts and phenomena, but also, first, the immediate and specific causes and principles and next, the deep-most, all-embracing springs from which the said facts and phenomena take their rise; in other words, a knowledge of thing and proximate cause; a knowledge of thing and ultimate cause.

Chapter Seven

The Genuine Intellectual

In philosophical jargon, a distinction is made between the *formal end* and the *final end* of any action or enterprise undertaken by a conscious agent. Here, however, to render what I am saying less esoteric or pedantic, I will simply speak of the End (for the formal end) and the Purpose (for the final end).

When I speak of the end of an action, I mean the natural obvious result that that action produces, in which it terminates; the end is external, objective, independent of the intention of the doer.

The purpose is the intention itself that the doer has in mind in doing what he does; it is entirely subjective.

When a person sharpens a knife, for instance, the natural, inevitable outcome is that the knife gets keen, sharp. But the intentions of two chaps sharpening knives may be miles apart; the purpose of one may be to carve up wood; that of the other may be to carve up a man, to cut a throat! Thus the end of an action, done as it should, with the means that ought to be employed, is invariable; whereas the intentions of the agents may be as different, one from the other, as sculpture is from murder. What, then, is the end of University Studies? The end of University studies is twofold

In the first place, university studies, correctly, diligently and thoroughly pursued, provide the student, in a specific-field, not with a formless heap of knowledge, like a random pile of stones, but with a corpus of facts and principles, a corpus of learning, which corpus shall have been built up, scientifically and philosophically, into a coherent, integrated, organised system, like a well-built house, or, better still, like a living organism. University studies, rightly and assiduously pursued, in other words, should provide, in a given domain, the expert, the technologist, the lawyer, the man of Letters, the chap skilled in mind, and, if need be, skilled in hand.

In the second place, by the prolonged, thorough, methodical that is, scientific and philosophical, exercise of his intellect on a particular field of university studies, the student should become instilled with a scientific and philosophical mind; – a mind whose natural reaction, when confronted with a phenomenon or problem, whatever it be, should be to dig to the proximate and the deep-most roots of the said problem or phenomenon; – a spirit that questions, that doubts, that searches, that inquires methodically, systematically; – a spirit that is not satisfied until it has unearthed the specific and proximate, the all-embracing and ultimate causes of things; a spirit ever thirsting for knowledge; a mind that never accepts as certain things unproved; – a mind and spirit whose watch-word is **Thorough**. In other words, correctly, diligently and thoroughly pursued, university studies should produce the thinker-scholar, or the individual that is more commonly referred to, in our day, as the **Intellectual**. Thus learning by rote, however profound the subject, can in no way be regarded as university education, properly so called.

The second aspect of the End of University Studies is of the highest importance. And, this, for various reasons.

Firstly, the thinker-scholar, or the scientist-philosopher, cannot seclude himself, forever, in the ivory tower of his specialisation. Life is not composed of water-tight compartments; and he will often, in private as well as in public life, come up against situations for which his particular field of studies offers no ready-made solutions. Indeed, it happens, very often, that fellows, after university studies, are called upon to serve in fields which have little or no bearing on what they did in college; and yet, even in this foreign field, they are expected to show proof of intellect and efficiency, by reason of their scientific and philosophical training. It is obvious then that the university man, irrespective of what his particular domain may be, will be looked up to, by virtue of his high education; indeed, it will even be incumbent on him to help to find answers to the manifold, diverse and often bailing and staggering questions that arise to confront the community in which he finds himself. This is so to the extent that Ralph Waldo Emerson, the American Philosopher (1803-1882) did not hesitate to make this seemingly exaggerated assertion: 'The scholar is that man who must take up into himself all the ability of the time, all the contributions of the past, all the hopes of the future. He must be a university of knowledges…'[12]

It is characteristic, therefore, of the genuine thinker-scholar, that however far-removed from his particular domain the problems he comes up against may be, he will approach and tackle them methodically, searchingly, with that scientific and philosophical spirit that years of drill in his special field have instilled into him; will search for all the relevant facts, for all the deep-most causes, will ponder them over, in order to draw out the conclusion that issues naturally, logically, from the said facts and causes.

There you have it – the twofold End of University Studies: it is, by long, thorough and diligent drilling to create in the mind concurrently, simultaneously, a corpus of knowledge built up scientifically and philosophically; and to inculcate into the mind a spirit which approaches and tackles every problem, whatever it be, scientifically,

---

12. Quoted in *Dialogue* (American Quarterly Journal) by Melvin J. Lasky, p. 30.

philosophically; in other words, University Studies should confer deep knowledge in a particular branch of learning, and, into the bargain, a sharp mind that questions, that wonders, that ponders, that digs to the depth of things.

The conclusion that University Studies should produce the thinker-scholar has led me to ask myself another question, namely, *what is an Intellectual?* For, today, the word is used so indiscriminately, so vaguely, so much out of rhyme and reason, that it is difficult without careful examination to say what the genuine intellectual is. What then are the qualities that make the thinker-scholar stand out, head and shoulders, above the general run of educated men and earn for him the title – Intellectual?

Let me begin by asking another question.

Suppose a chap, after a brilliant university career, gets a job, let us say, as a civil servant, and piles his skills superbly, and becomes an expert *back-room boy,* an efficient executive of policies handed down to him by his political bosses; but suppose he never thinks to give himself pause to ponder and wonder whether these policies and the rules that govern their execution stem from expediency or from fundamental principle; whether, inherently, they are good and right or evil and wrong, whether they will lead, in the long run, to the weal or to the woe of the commonwealth, in order to warn his masters of impending catastrophe; suppose he gets into the rut of unthinking routine, reads nothing but files, never looks beyond the narrow confines of his civil service job to see the world without; but employs superb intelligence to justify ready-made policies and to make them work. – would such a man be called an intellectual, even if he were endowed with a mind sharp and keen and was armed with a doctorate?

I say no.

What then are the hall-marks of the authentic intellectual as distinguished from the merely highly intelligent man?

The first is that, in the genuine intellectual, mind reigns supreme, at least in so far as things that lie within the realm of reason are concerned; he possesses not merely highly specialised knowledge in a given field but is dominated by that scientific and philosophical spirit of which I have spoken above. Obviously, no man, on this imperfect earth, is pure mind. Even the most mentally endowed will be impeded by his inborn temperament, the stem and background from which he sprung, the *milieu* in which he was reared, with all that these entail of sentiment, tradition, prejudice, bias. Yet, as I have said already, the first characteristic of the genuine intellectual is that, in him, in spite of these, mind will reign and rule supreme; in him it shall be, ever his guiding light, his final arbiter, his chief justice, his lord and king.

The second characteristic of the genuine intellectual is that, consequent on this supremacy and primacy of mind in him, his main preoccupation, his predominant, all-absorbing concern in life shall be the *search for the Truth*. As Truth's votary, ever faithful, ever sure, he is committed to wage life-long warfare against falsehood. And as goodness and beauty are inherent in truth, it follows that he must be a constant seeker of the good and right and an inexorable and implacable foe of evil and wrong; and a devoted worshipper at the shrine of the beautiful and the sublime.

Since the depths of Truth are unfathomable, since Goodness is boundless, since the riches of Beauty are inexhaustible, it follows that the real intellectual must be a diligent student all his days. So complex is the universe, so complex and inscrutable the life of man, that there is no field of learning, however narrow, where men can confidently say that they have seen the last. Thus, the moment he says good-bye to his books and ceases to inquire, and ceases to reflect, and ceases to focus a searching light into his own soul, and ceases to question the status quo critically, he ceases, *ipso facto,* to be an intellectual. His university career, rightly understood, is only a springboard from which to plunge ever deeper into the mysteries of his own special field, into the depth of truth at large.

Furthermore, if intellect is to reign and rule supreme in the thinker-scholar, if his search for. the True, the Good and Beautiful is to keep along the right road, if his thinking is to remain pure and straight, if his spirit is to shine like a lambent light in limpid atmosphere, his mind must be keen, cold firm, serene, above bias, above prejudice, above passion. For heated passion and pride and prejudice deprive the thinker of discipline and control, becloud the mind and warp judgment; they are the deadliest foes of intellectual life. Thus, it is easy to perceive that this keenness, this coldness, this serenity, this firmness of mind are of the utmost importance in the thinker-scholar. For the intellectual is Seer and Prophet, the eye and mind of society; and, to assume this awful role efficiently, and to the full, he must be able to see both deep and far, must have both insight and foresight, in order to recognise, as some wits have put it, not merely ideas that have arrived, but also ideas whose time has not yet come; in order, when the need arises, to warn his community of coming catastrophe. The genuine intellectual, therefore, is a diligent, dispassionate, unrelenting searcher, a deep and foresighted seer, the mind and eye of society, its humble, persuasive, faithful, unsubservient servant; not a haughty bigoted, self-styled prophet, contemptuous of the crowd, denouncing the weak, and predicting doom.

For, indeed the deeper genuine learning and 'scholarship penetrate, the more they should induce a profound and ever deepening humility. For, as I have stressed already, the universe is complex, and complex is the nature and the life of man. Each tiniest section, each tiniest detail, that we take up to investigate, however infinitesimal it may seem, is a labyrinthal and unexhaustible world in itself. There is hardly any thesis however logical, however lofty, propounded and defended by an eminent philosopher, that has not been attacked and denounced by another philosopher equally eminent. Truth is intricate and elusive. The portion of the universe, or of the life of man, about which men can speak with categorical certitude, is small when compared with the vast Unknown. Most of the ideas, that men of learning and thought propound and propose, are, at best, opinions or hypotheses to be held and used while research continues to unearth new facts which may come either to confirm and consolidate the said opinions and hypotheses, or to disprove and reject them. Indeed it has been said of the really learned man that the more he learns, the more he learns that he knows nothing. Within even his special field, no scientist or philosopher or expert can lay claim to omniscience and infallibility. How much more when he ventures out of it? Within or without his special field he has to search assiduously, meticulously, to dig deep, to pile relevant fact on relevant fact, cogent principle on cogent principle, in order to draw conclusions, cautious, yes, but solid enough to enable him to proceed with firm foot, and, if need be, to speak with a sure degree of authority. Thus no intellectual, genuinely such, will dare to assume the posture of a sovereign pontiff, speaking *ex cathedra* and hurling anathemas on those who differ or disagree. Indeed rigid dogmatism is one of the surest signs of a shallow mind. Yet the stance of the intellectual on a point that has been the object of diligent and meticulous study and probing, on his part, should be neither timid nor apologetic; having gathered all the relevant facts he can dig up, all the principles relative to the point, having drawn the logical, cogent conclusion that issues inevitably from the said facts and principles, he should speak with confidence, yes, even with authority; but ever with the humble readiness to correct his stand, should new facts and principles come to light, to prove him wrong.

On a par with, yes, even more important than, humble open-mindedness, as an authentic hall-mark of the thinker-scholar, is his intellectual and moral independence. Intellectually, his mind should not become the slave of any established, dogmatic system, however coherent, however cogent, however excellent, yes, however sacred they may look; for the human mind, in the nature of things, is limited, man's nature is corrupt, and, thus, when things hallowed are entrusted to men, they will vitiate them, inevitably; through their weakness of mind; through the natural drag towards evil that is part and parcel of our nature; through narrowness, pride and bigotry. As thinker and critic, the intellectual must stand back, detached, and scrutinise, and ponder, and evaluate; and accept or reject things on their intrinsic merit, on principle and conviction. If he is faithful to his calling, he cannot become the victim of unthinking routine, or a mindless cog in the wheel of any Establishment, whatsoever. To gain and consolidate his moral inde-pendence, the intellectual should shun, indeed, should wage unrelenting ceaseless war, against the enticements of a life of ease, against the allurements of wealth, and, most especially, against the insidious seductions of power. In its sublimest form, intellectual ism will condemn its devoted, uncompromising votary to the life of a loner. Schiller wrote and Beethoven sang, inviting all men to participate in universal joy. This *Hymn to Joy* singles out as the foremost invitees:

> *Wem der grosse Wurf ge lunge n, eines Freundes Freund zu sein; wer ein holdes Weib errungen, mische seinen Jubel ein!*
> He who has got the good fortune to be the friend of a friend; he who has won a worthy wife, let him join the jubilee![13]

---

13. Fricdrick Schiller's *An die Freude* (Hymn to Joy), immortalised by Ludwig van Beethoven in his *Choral* or *Nineth Symphony*.

The poet's words rendered immortal by the genius of one of the greatest music-makers the world has ever seen, are true and beautiful and profound; and the genuine intellectual must be the ardent lover and servant of the human kind, the affectionate brother of every human being. Yet the conscientious thinker-scholar of the highest worth must be wary of certain human contacts and shield himself resolutely against relationships likely to lead to betrayal of principle or vicious compromise. Detached thinker and critic, jealous of his independence, the intellectual of this worth and calibre will find himself, more often than not, at variance with society, will be sometimes bound to reprove, will risk hostility and rejection and will often be forced to walk a lonesome road. In an imperfect world, the devoted thinker-scholar dedi-cated to the defence of the ideal, is bound, more often than not, to be a non-conformist. As one writer put it: 'The *intellectual* is the natural guardian of quality in the life of the mind and the natural critic of shoddy. He is the partisan of the ideal. That is why, if he is faithful to his calling in the imperfect world and culture in which he lives, he cannot become the poet laureate of the status quo.'[14]

This will often arouse indignation and draw upon his head the fury and thunder, especially, of men in power with a stake in the system he calls to question. Yet this critical attitude of the committed thinker-scholar, this non-conformism, is not the bane but the boon of man, will lead not to the woe but to the weal of society. Students of American political history will agree with me that hardly any politician in recent times did more than the late Adlai Stevenson to bring thought into the ruthless arena of American politics. Although he failed twice in his bid for the highest office, he won a significant moral victory in that

---

14. The Philosopher Sidney Hook, quoted in Dialogue with Vol. 1, No. 2, p. 33.

formidable philistinism of the American political establishment and ushered thought and mind into the public affairs of the U.S.A. On this point, Stevenson himself left a statement worthy of note: 'The conformists abominate thought. Thinking implies disagreement and disagreement implies non-confor-mity and non-conformity implies heresy and heresy implies disloyalty. So obviously thinking must be stopped... But I say to you that bawling is not a substitute for thinking and that reason is not the subversion but the salvation of freedom.'[15]

When I look back into the vista of History, and ask myself whom I rate, in my judgment, as the greatest intellectual, in the highest sense of the term, the world has ever seen, that stands out, in the lengthy panorama of the human story, as a giant colossus, dwarfing all others; the detached, independent, dedicated, keen-minded thinker, profound in thought, shorn of ambition, abstemious, large-hearted; the gad-fly and goad of society, ever stinging, ever prodding, at his risk and peril, to urge men towards Truth and Goodness – when I ask myself this question, I would (barring Christ, not to get involved in the question of his Godhead) unhesitating single out Socrates, the ever-questioning philosopher of ancient Athens, whose name has become a house-hold word, from his day to this. He took his calling so seriously, brought it through so thoroughly that he finally aroused the furious Athenians and they hurried him before the court to try him for his life. The court pronounced him guilty of death, but before he died this is what he said, among other things:

> I have never lived an ordinary quiet life. I did not care for the things that most people care about; making money, having a comfortable home, high military or civil rank, and all the other activities – political

---

15. Vol. l.No. 2, p. 14.

appointments, secret societies, party organisations – which go on in our city; I thought that I was really too strict in my principles to survive if I went in for this sort of thing. So instead of taking a course which would have done no good either to you or to me, I set myself to do you individually in private what I hold to be the greatest possible service: I tried to persuade each one of you not to think more of practical advantages than of his mental and moral well-being...

It is literally true (even if it sounds rather comical) that God has specially appointed me to this city, as though it were a large thoroughbred horse which because of its great size is inclined to be lazy and needs the stimulation of some stinging fly. It seems to me that God has attached me to this city to perform the office of such a fly; and all day long I never cease to settle here, there, and everywhere, rousing, persuading, reproving every one of you. You will not easily fine another like me, gentlemen, and if you take my advice you will spare my life. I suspect, however, that before long you will awake from your drowsing, and in your annoyance you will take Anytus' advice and finish me off with a single slap; and then you will go on sleeping till the end of your days, unless God in his care for you sends someone to take my place.

If you doubt whether I am really the sort of person who would have been sent to this city as a gift from God, you can convince yourselves by looking at it in this way. Does it seem natural that I should have neglected my own affairs and endured the humiliation of allowing my family to be neglected for all these years, while I busied myself all the time on your behalf, going like a father or an elder brother to see each one of you privately, and urging you to set your thoughts on goodness? If I had got any enjoyment from it, or if I had been paid for my good advice, there would have been some explanation for my conduct, but as it is, you can see for yourselves that although my accusers unblushingly charge me with all sorts of other crimes, there is one thing that they have not had the impudence to pretend on any testimony, and that is that I have ever exacted or asked a fee from anyone. The witness that I can offer to prove the truth of my statement is, I think, a convincing one – my poverty.[16]

If the intellectual, as I have defined him, is to be unflinchingly faithful to his role, that is, to be the untiring seeker of the true, the – good, the right and the beautiful and their dauntless defender against falsehood, evil, injustice and Philistinism; if he is to be the principled non-conformist, or as I have baptised him, the gadfly and goad of society, risking 'the frown of the great', and 'the tyrant's stroke;' he must acquire a will of granite, must possess or cultivate a more than normal calibre of courage. Indeed, without fearlessness, without the readiness to die, to lose all if need be, no thinker-scholar, however high his talent, can ever make an impact on his community. In my view, nobody, in our times, understood this more than Mahatma Gandhi, who, in a fashion out of this world, played in modern India a role similar to that which Socrates played in ancient Athens. To steel himself for this vocation, Gandhi took some stringent, indeed almost unearthly vows, foremost among which were the Vow of Truth and the Vow of Fearlessness:

> Not simply truth, he said, as we ordinarily understand it, not truth which merely answers the saying 'Honesty is the best Policy', implying that if it is not the best policy we may depart from it, Here Truth as it is conceived means that we may have to rule our life by this law of Truth at any cost; and in order to satisfy the definition, I have drawn upon the celebrated

---

16. Plato: *The Apology*, p.p. 43-44; 36-37; translated by Hugh Tredenick, the Penguin Classics, 1957.

illustration of the life of Prahlad. For the sake of Truth he dared to oppose his own father; and he defended himself, not by paying his father back in his own coin. Rather, in defence of Truth as he knew it, he was prepared to die without caring to return the blows that he had received from his father, or from those who were charged with his father's instructions. Not only that, he would not in any way even parry the blows; on the contrary, with a smile on his lips, he underwent the innumerable tortures to which he was subjected, with the results that at last Truth rose triumphant. Not that he suffered the tortures because he knew that some day or other in his very lifetime he would be able to demonstrate the infallibility of the Law of Truth. That fact was there; but if he had died in the midst of tortures he would still have adhered to Truth. That is the Truth which I would like to follow. In our Ashram we make it a rule that we must say 'No' when we mean No, regardless of consequences.

I found, through my wanderings in India, that my country is seized with a paralysing fear. We may not open our lips in public; we may only talk about our opinions secretly. We may do anything we like within the four walls of our house; but those things are not for public consumption.

If we had taken a vow of silence I would have nothing to say. I suggest to you that there is only One whom we have to fear, that is God. When we fear God, then we shall fear no man, however high-placed he may be; and if you want to follow the vow of Truth, then fearlessness is absolutely necessary. Before we can aspire to guide the destinies of India we shall have to adopt this habit of fearlessness.[17]

---

17. ANDREWS, C.F., *Mahatma Gandhi's ideas*, p.p. 102, 103, 108, George Alien and Unwin, 1947.

I have said that it is of the highest importance that the thinker-scholar should possess a cold mind; I also say that it is of equally highest importance that he should possess a warm heart; should be a man who, by loving his neighbours, by loving his community, by loving those in need, loves mankind at large; is concerned about its welfare, rejoices in its triumphs and grieves at its tragedies. For one of the frightening spectacles of the modern world is that, as science becomes more and more powerful, and takes over labour, and conquers the universe, and attains the stars; as ideologies wax more furious with exclusive bigotry; as political ambitions become increasingly staggering, man, the individual, is counting for less and less; he has virtually ceased to be a **human being** and has become a **number** – just one among a nameless, faceless, countless mammoth multitude. Take the case, for instance, of the head of a mighty state waging war, with specious motives; does it ever occur to him as he listens to the news and hears the piling figures of the dead announced, monotonously, day after day, does it occur to him that each man killed is an irreparable loss, means deep personal grief to a large number of friends and relatives? Maybe it does. But this butchery, perpetrated every day, becoming commonplace, has come to look as rather in the nature of things; and we are getting ages away from President Lincoln who sat down to write his historic letter to a mother who had lost five sons in the Civil War. This war told on him, wore him down, because he felt for men. No, man hardly counts any more. But, to the true intellectual, he should count, before all else; should be his prime preoccupation. That is why the question he should be asking himself, ceaselessly, with regard to his special field is: How can I use my studies to promote the welfare of man? what contribution can I make, by virtue of my trained mind, to solve the problems that beset my community, to give man's life a purpose, and help to achieve that purpose?

Yes, man, first and last, should be the foremost concern of the genuine intellectual. Thus one of the most outstanding hall-marks of the authentic thinker-scholar is that he is a humanist, in the purest sense of the term. Thus, scientific and philosophical learning, a scientific and philosophical mind are not ends in themselves; the academy, the university, is only a cultivating ground, a manufactory, a store house from where we cull ideas for the furtherance of the well-being of man; a training camp for the future fighters for human freedom. And knowledge and a cultivated mind are but means and weapons for the achievement of this manward purpose. 'Men in high intellectual enterprise', said the physicist, Robert Oppenheimer, 'must contribute to the common culture, where we talk to each other, not just about – the facts of nature. . . but about the nature of the human predicament, about the nature of man, about law, about the good and the bad, about morality, about political virtue, about politics in the Aristotelian sense.'[18]

Primacy and Predominance of intellect, therefore, devotion and fidelity to the True, the Good and the Beautiful, an insatiate thirst for knowledge, life-long devotion to its quest, intellectual detachment and independence, indifference and immunity to the enticements of pleasure, wealth and power, humble openness of mind, a will of steel, a fearless heart, deep concern for the fate of man these are, at least, among the foremost qualities of the genuine intellectual

---

18. Quoted in *Dialogue,* Vol. 1, No. 2, p. 25.

Chapter Eight

Dedication To The Common Weal

I said at the start of the last chapter that, whereas the end of an action or enterprise is the natural, inevitable objective outcome that issues from the said action or enterprise, the purpose, on the other hand, is the subjective intention that the doer has in mind in doing what he does; the end should be invariable, constant; the purpose for the most part is various, differing from person to person.

When I first went to University, as I have said already, I noticed that most of the boys and girls I met there had for their foremost purpose to snatch a degree and get a job, as soon as possible, thereafter. By and large, this is the prominent and prevalent intent almost everywhere, especially in the rising countries where a good and high education is one of the surest means of social and economic preferment. You see it in a country like ours where the French mentality has given rise to a veritable cult of degrees; a green-horn returning from a University or from an *Haute Ecole* in France with titles fit to fill half a page, nourishes the ambition, before he has hardly taken his seat behind a desk, to be nominated *directeur* of this or *chef de service* of that; and will lobby and even intrigue to achieve this end; and become disgruntled and bitter if he fails in his bid. Prove their worth first, by a competent, skilful, conscientious and impressive prolonged performance of a task – few give a thought to that. Merely because they are armed with a string of degrees, they would feel insulted if anyone dared to suggest that that is not enough; that they need, into the bargain, to acquire expertise and experience and vindicate their worth and impose themselves by a few years of diligent, competent exercise, and by acquiring the knack of handling men and the skilful ability to govern and to guide. In like manner most parents with a son in University look upon his presence there, purely and simply, as a financial investment which should begin to bring in dividends as soon as the student leaves the campus and gets a job. Furthermore, in present-day Africa, when politicians lay the foundation-stone of a new university, at the lowest, they have an eye on the next elections, on consolidating themselves in office thereby; at best, they are anxious to furnish the services of the State with a corps of expert personnel, or, to use a much-worn expression in French-speaking Africa, they are intent on furthering *la formation de cadres*.

These are some of the current reasons why young men and women seek university education, why parents, if they can, stint themselves to keep a son on the campus, why governments, especially in the new countries, set up universities. There is nothing wrong with these reasons; yet, they are low, self-centred, circumscribed and fall short of the ideal

What then should be the lofty, large and selfless purpose that educators should have ever in mind in imparting university learning?

Obviously, the End of University Studies, of which I have spoken so much above, that is, the formation of men armed with deep systematised knowledge in a specific field, men equipped, consequently, with a scientific and philosophical bent of mind, that is, the production of the genuine thinker-scholar, the scientist-philosopher, in short, the production of the authentic intellectual, should constitute, in itself, and at once, a primary purpose of university education.

Yet the intellectual, thus conceived and fashioned, however brilliant, however skilful, however profound in science and scholarship, does not constitute an end in himself; you do not produce him merely for the pleasure of producing him, to set him up (for popular worship) like a golden calf in the wilderness of ignorance and mediocrity. The pertinent question is: what should he do with his learning and skill and mind; to what use should he put his specialised knowledge, his scientific and philosophical training? In other words, what should be the ultimate purpose for providing a given community, or society at large, with the university trained man – the scientist, the technologist, the thinker-scholar, the genuine intellectual?

I have pondered this question over and over again, and, ever I have come to one and the same conclusion, namely, that the purpose of university education should be, not merely to equip the rising youth with scientific and philosophical knowledge and skill and mind, but most especially to instil into them, over and above, a deep, keen and lofty sense of dedication to the service of the commonwealth, the immediate community of which they are members, and thereby, to the service of the world as a whole, of humanity at large.

But how should this sense of dedication and service be manifested, how should it be put into effect in the concrete; or, to put it more generally, what roles, what services, should a genuine intellectual perform among men?

The most obvious and immediate one is that he should put his special knowledge or skill (as an agronomist, an engineer, an economist, a social scientist, an educationist, a philosopher) at the disposal of the community. But this is not enough. To whom much has been given, from him much shall be required. And the university man out of academy and among ordinary men would be a woeful failure if he did no more than ply his special skill. What then is required of him over and above?

Firstly, I have said earlier that the genuine intel-lectual should regard his university studies essentially as a springboard from which to plunge deeper still and deeper into the bottomless waters of knowledge; that he must remain a student, a researcher, a thinker all his days. The essential intention here is that these studies, this research, this thinking should result not merely in increased learning, on his part, for himself, but in the discovery of new knowledge for the humankind – a new fact, a new thought, a new principle, a new law. Thus the foremost and never-ending role of the intellectual is to be a seeker who finds, who discovers. As finder or discoverer he causes the horizons of knowledge to recede further back; he sets the bounds of learning wider still and wider, by adding something more, something new, to the existing store of human science and wisdom.

Secondly, thanks to the finding of new facts, new thought, new laws, new principles, the scientist-philosopher builds up new solutions, concrete or abstract, for the problems that face his community or the world at large. In this way, like a man who fathers a son, he participates in the unending act by which God is ceaselessly creating and renewing the world. By such singular and original accomplishment, the scientist-philosopher, the thinker-scholar, the genuine intellectual, becomes a creator, a maker. To this category of makers obviously belong the great benefactors of mankind who have invented sources of energy, new tools to make labour easier, speedier, more efficient, most prolific; and life more liveable; who are creating or perfecting new means, new machines to make travel ever swifter, ever surer; to make communication more instant and clearer and, thereby, bring the far-flung peoples of the world closer and closer, together.

But special mention must be made of that class of creators who dedicate their talents to the finding of solutions to the inner problems that plague the human kind, and, thus contribute to the continued moral and spiritual enrichment and renewal of society. Such are the thinkers and philosophers whose works of unprecedented originality, depth and power have made revolutions and changed or reshaped the course of history and the face of the world. You see them standing out like giant land-marks in the long-drawn vista of the story and progress of man. As an example in modern times towers the colossus Marx. But there have been others without number, in all places, at all times, who, though less gigantic, have contributed effectively, by their thought, in the making of a better human being and of a world fitter to live in.

Here also must be mentioned that class of creative thinkers who have not merely been content to address themselves to a coterie of the initiate, but have also sought to reach the ordinary man by presenting their thought to him in concrete, living, dramatic shape. They dig deep down into the depths of the human soul, into the heart of society, in order to discover the root sources and springs of their behaviour, in order to grasp their inmost nature and workings; then they proceed to mirror or depict the world of their day as it really, truly and deeply is, with its joys and sorrows; its problems, its perplexities, its dilemmas, its conflicts; its triumphs, its blunders, its tragedies, catastrophes; and, through, seductive media – history, the novel, the play, the short story, the fable, the poem, the essay – these creative writers propose effective solutions to these problems, either for the individual, or for mankind at large. Indeed, makers of great literature are **creative** intellectuals in the truest sense of the term; for from their studies and research, from their meditations, from their own souls, from the intimate experience of their own lives, from their penetrating observation and insight into the world of their times, they create a new and similar world and people it with men and women who live intensely and love and laugh and come to grief and suffer and perish. Thus, makers of creative literature, by rewarding virtue and punishing vice and waywardness, strive to show how life on earth ought to be lived, how a measure of real happiness can be attained. At its less ambitious, creative literature strives at catharsis, strives to purge and soothe the emotions and give suffering humanity a brief escape and respite from the dreary drudgery and monotony of real life in this weary world.

In this effort to reach and instruct the ordinary man at large, the thinker-scholar participates directly in the achievement of a fundamental end and purpose of intellectual enterprise, namely, the creation of an **Intellectual Public**; a public alert, enlightened, disciplined and sagacious and firm in decision and action. For knowledge must penetrate the masses, must illuminate minds, and stir up wills and wisely rouse to action, if it is to change society and the world – for the better.

Furthermore, the thinker-scholar, thanks to his special training and knowledge; thanks to his scientific and philosophical bent of mind; thanks to his ceaseless searchings into his own soul, the endless questioning of his own life; thanks to his penetrating insight into the labyrinthal nature of the soul of man, into the mazes and the intricate workings of the nature of society; thanks to his comprehensive knowledge of the past, becomes a **Seer** into the confusing depths of the human mind, into the illusive future, a **Light** in the darkness of his days urging men towards right and rewarding achievement and rich fulfilment; or warning society, should the need arise, against impending cataclysm. Seer and Light, he *ipso facto* becomes a teacher, not in the sense of a pontiff expounding dogma, or a priest propounding mystery and pre-occupied with ritual, but in the sense of a humble persuader who 'shows the light', as Zik's motto once ran, for the people to find the way; who imposes himself on his community by the force of his logic; by the profundity of his scholarship, his insight and foresight;

his clarity of thought, his precision of expression; the transparence of his sincerity, his rectitude and integrity; who imposes himself by the shining example of his life.

This to my mind is the surest way by which the thinker-scholar, the man of Letters can help to transform a mindless, heedless community into that intellectual public, the creation of which intellectual public should constitute the foremost purpose of his endeavours.

I now come to a point, which, as I see it, is of the first and highest importance. It is this. If the thinker-scholar is verily a Seer, one of the foremost things on which he will inescapably, relentlessly, have to focus the searching light of his eye and mind will be on the nature of good and evil, of right and wrong, of justice and injustice, in the living of private lives, in the conduct of public affairs; and, since man is corrupt from conception, helpless at the enticements and the seductions of evil, more often than not; more inclined to wrong than to right, to injustice than to fairness; since the holders of office, the wielders of power, will be tempted more surely, more irresistibly, to its abuse than to its judicious and salutary use; the genuine thinker-scholar, if he is faithful, if he is *integer vitae scelerisque purus*[19] – pure of life and free from sin – he must become, inevitably, the *Keeper of the Public Conscience;* indeed he will have to be the very Conscience itself of Society. If he is really genuine, far from being a cynical, supercilious, haughty, self-righteous, self-appointed judge of weak and erring men, he will become a humble votary of Truth, Goodness and Justice: ever conscious of his own weaknesses and short-comings, full of sympathetic understanding; but yet a determined, unflinching, dauntless combatant in the war of truth against falsehood, of good against evil, of right against wrong, of justice against injustice, of humaneness against wickedness,

---

19. HORACE: Lib. 1- Car. XXII.

of freedom against tyranny; he will become a tireless crusader-persuader urging men by word and deed along the road to right; a goad and gadfly, ever pricking, ever stinging society in order to rouse its conscience to shun evil and seek the good; a fearless defender of truth and justice ever ready to front 'the frown of the great,' to bide 'the tyrant's stroke.'

Now I come to another point at once provocative and controversial but, to my mind of capital relevance and urgency, especially in emerging Africa. Here it is. Should the specialist, the technologist, the scientist-philosopher, the thinker-scholar, the intellectual (whichever you please) participate in the conception of policy, in its implementation, in the running of the State? To put it in less scholarly jargon: should the intellectual take part in politics?

My answer is unhesitating and unequivocal: Yes.

And saying yes with me are some of the highest authorities the world has ever seen.

For his part Socrates laid it down categorically, without mincing words, that those destined to rule, should be given, as an absolute prerequisite, a thorough physical, moral and intellectual education.[20]

For his part, Aristotle asserted tersely that 'A good State IF not the work of Fortune but of Knowledge and Purpose; a state is good only when those citizens who have a share in the government are themselves good'.[21]

Plato is celebrated for his famous dictum that either philosophers must be kings or kings philosophers: 'Unless' said he, 'philosophers bear kingly rule in cities, or those who are now called kings and princes become genuine and adequate philosophers, and political power and philosophy are brought together, and unless the numerous natures who

---

20. *Socratic Discourses,* Xenophon (and Plato), Everyman's Library, No. 457, Book 1. Chapter VI; Book 2, Chapter I.
21. Aristotle: *Politics, ibid.* No. 605, Book VII, p. 210.

at present pursue either politics or philosophy, the one to the exclusion of the other, are forcibly debarred from this behaviour, there will be no respite from evil, my dear Glaucon, for cities, nor, I fancy, humanity. . .'[22]

Indeed, who can doubt it, who can challenge it and still lay claim to truth and honesty, namely, that there is need for the best efforts of the best minds in the conception and the running of public affairs?

On the other hand, intellectualism tends to lift men away from the crude, brute world into the high ethereal heavens of lofty absolute principles. Partici-pation in affairs of state brings them back to earth, and sobers them down, and chastens them by putting them at grips with the dangerous, bewildering, care-needing, nerve-racking task of the governance and guidance of erring men – by erring men.

But in what ways should he do this? What role should the intellectual play in the running of public affairs?

The first is an obvious one, albeit indirect, namely, where men of intelligence (even of intellect) and specialised training – experts, technologists - serve in the civil service as executors of policy or advisers to government - the faceless, self-effacing men of know-how that, in England, people refer to, mockingly, as *back-room boys*. Under a politician who respects expertise, or one who, on the contrary, does not understand what the whole thing is all about and lets the experts to their job, these faceless boys behind the scenes can wield tremendous power. Conversely, under conceited, wayward, wrong-headed ruthless politicians, who believe they know all about it and don't need to be told, the intellectual, in this role, is in real trouble. And, if he is not firm of mind and will, he will constantly be harassed and plagued by the fear of rousing the fury of his boss, of losing his job.

---

22. Plato: *The Republic, ibid*, No. 64, Book V, p. 166.

What is worse, sometimes, intellectuals in this position fall victim to the seductions of greed, and degrade themselves into yes-men, sycophants, servile flatterers, opportunists, for whom preferment be-comes the *summum bonum,* the sole and single ambition, for which all self-respect and integrity should be sacrificed. *Conuptio optimi pessima,* says a Latin adage – the corruption of the best is the worst; there is hardly any degradation so deep, so unsightly, as that of an intellectual who prostitutes his talent and himself so meanly. Thus it is clear that the intellectual in this position will often need guts to see to it that his expert knowledge is not used to serve expediency or to achieve outright evil ends. There is no denying that given the chance and the green light, if he is honest in mind, firm of will, faithful to truth and principle, and dedicated to the public weal, the expert thinker-scholar, even in this role of playing second fiddle, can do a world of good to promote sound government.

But another question remains to be cleared; to wit, should intellectuals participate in public affairs as politicians on their own right?

Here answers are hesitant.

There are those who, seeing what power politics have to warp and debase even the best-intentioned of men, espouse the thesis that the genuine intellectual, Socrates-wise, should stay clean out of his corrupting, often sordid, enterprise; that he should remain a nay-saying outsider, uncompromising defender of the ideal. Indeed, when one has seen how rotten politics can be, how rank with expediency, lying, ruthlessness, Philistinism, treachery, run-away ambition, and what have you, one is powerfully drawn to agree with the protagonists of this view.

Still I persist in the belief that it is necessary, even imperative that, at least, some intellectuals should steel their will and brace themselves and enter the arena of politics in order to usher in and further thought and conscience and righteousness and integrity in the conduct of public affairs. On this point I am in full agreement with an American Congressman with a Harvard-Oxford background who had this to say:

> I think. . . that in political life we need both men of intelligence and men of intellect; for in politics, as in every other field, we must have 'intelligent' men who are capable of operating 'within the framework of limited but clearly started goals.' But just as we need 'intelligent' men in politics, in both the executive and legislative branches, we also need some 'intellectual' men. That is to say, we need persons who are willing to evaluate the evaluations, to raise questions about the policies themselves as well as the methods for implementing policies, willing, indeed, to inquire into the presuppositions on the basis of which policies are made.

Politics – even electoral politics – requires more than first-class technicians, indispensable as these are. If our society is to remain open and free, if it is not to stumble and falter when confronted with the enormous problems we face, there must be in decision-making positions in our government – in Congress – and not only as advisers but as principals, at least some men who are deeply concerned with objectives and assumptions as well as with techniques and methods. There must be some men who are interested in rethinking policy as well as explaining it, interested not only in making present policies work, but in asking whether they are right. There must be at least some politicians who do not feel threatened with complexity, but challenged and stimulated by it.

To view the status quo critically and not simply to be its servant is, I believe, the appropriate role of the intellectual in politics as well as out of it. He may finally decide – or he may not – to attack established policy; as an intellectual, however, his chief vocation is to scrutinize it.

... there are many... ways of improving the exchange of ideas between the political and intellectual communities. The final one, of course, is for more thoughtful, well-educated men and women to become candidates for Congress; more citizens of intellect and intelligence to become politicians. Young men and women with con-victions about the direction in which their country should move will find in Congress an opportunity to assert these convictions and thereby serve the public.

... there is a satisfaction in being involved, even with but one voice and vote, in decisions that shape the future of the country and the world.[23]

But in entering the lists to joust for thought and right in the political tournament, as an active participant, in his own right, the scientist-philosopher, the thinker-scholar, the intellectual must bear one thing ever in mind. It is that he is now in the domain, not of the **Absolute**, but in that of the **Possible**; that he is in a field in which dialogue and negotiation and judicious compromise are the watch-words. I insist on the term judicious compromise advisedly, because I do not intend, in the least, that compromise should cloak a betrayal of inalienable principle. In the rough and tumble of politics, the intellectual, dedicated to the Ideal, will have to learn to temper his Idealism with deep-sighted Realism. As I see it, the Realist-Idealist is one who, while keeping his ideal ever before the eye of his mind, while knowing thoroughly that core and essence of it that cannot be bargained away, that cannot even be made the subject of negotiation, is yet practical and shrewd enough to know exactly how much of his ideal he can realise *hic et nunc*, here and now, in present concrete circumstances; who knows the marginal non-essentials that he can sacrifice to conditions of time and "place, without betrayal of the substance of principle.

---

23. *Dialogue: Vol.* 7. No, 2, pp. 11-12, 21, 22.

Yet, in this hurly-burly, the thinker-scholar should never forget that his foremost, utmost, inmost purpose in life, as an intellectual, is to think, even for thinking's sake; should never forget that his essential mission in politics is to be the Conscience and not merely the Agent of society; that, on no account should he become, merely and simply, the apologist of the status quo. Henry Kissinger,* once Harvard don, now special adviser to President Nixon, had this to say on this point: 'The intellectual should not refuse to participate in policy-making, for to do so would confirm administrative stagnation. But in cooperating. . . it is important for him to remember that one of his contributions to the administrative process is his independence, and that one of his tasks is to seek to prevent unthinking routine from becoming an end in itself.'[24]

Thus, from my point of sight, some intellectuals, at least, should become sharers of power, direct parti-cipants in active politics. I say some advisedly, because I still believe, firmly, that, in society, in so far as politics are concerned, there is an essential, permanent need for the intellectual outsider – that votary of Truth, that defender of the Ideal who is untrammelled by partisan considerations, who has no eye on the next elections, no heart on office. Such men have been 'the salt of the earth', as Christ put it, the shapers and changers of the world, – men like Socrates, Plato and Aristotle, in days of long ago, like Marx and Gandhi in modern times.

To summarise what I have been saying on this head, I can do no better than put before the reader the learned views that were expressed on this point by the famous English university Churchman and scholar, John Henry Cardinal Newman:

---

* Publisher's Note: When Jimmy Carter won the Democratic elections into the Presidency in 1976, Kissinger was replaced by Cirus Vancc.

24. *Ibid*, Vol. 7. No. 2, p. 17.

Necessity has no law, and expedience is often one form of necessity. It is no principle with sensible men, of whatever cast of opinion, to do always what is abstractedly best. Where no direct duty forbids, we may be obliged to do, as being best under circumstances, what we murmur and rise against, while we do it. We see that to attempt more is to effect less; that we must accept so much, or gain nothing; and so perforce we reconcile ourselves to what we would have far otherwise, if we could. . .

I allow them fully, that, when men combine together for any common object, they are obliged as a matter of course, in order to secure the advantages accruing from united action, to sacrifice many of their private opinions and wishes and to drop the minor differences, as they .are commonly called, which exist between man and man. No two persons perhaps are to be found, however intimate, however congenial in tastes and judgments, however eager to have one heart and one soul, but must deny themselves, for the sake of each other, much which they like or desire, if they are to live together happily. Compromise, in a large sense of the word, is the first principle of combination; and anyone who insists on enjoying his rights to the full, and his opinions without toleration for his neighbour's, and his own way in all things will soon have all things altogether to himself, and no one to share them with him. But most true as this confessedly is, still there is an obvious limit, on the other hand, to these compromises, necessary as they are; and this is found in the proviso, that the differences surrendered should be but 'minor', or that there should be no sacrifice of the main object of the combination, in the concessions which are mutually made. Any

> sacrifice which compromises that object is destructive of the principle of the combination, and no one who would be consistent can be a part to it.[25]

Such being the characteristic of the genuine intellectual – his dedication to the Ideal, to mind and meditation, his obligation to tell the truth as it is, his non-conformism, his role as critic of society, as Keeper of the Public Conscience – an interesting rider to consider is, what have been the attitudes towards intellectuals in various places and at various times. Let us begin with the most favourable – apparently.

To begin with, it is that of those who worship the intellectuals and rain on them showers of fulsome praise. Any genuine thinker-scholar shrinks back with horror from adulation as from the plague, runs away from fans as from a 'madding crowd.' Back in 1962, I attended a conference of African writers of English expression in Makerere, Kampala, Uganda. This conference warned the rising African writers against the exaggerated praise poured on them by European admirers – well-meaning people, but who, burning with thirst for the strange and exotic, seize on the budding efforts of the African writers and laud them to the skies as if they were the very quintessence of human achievement; whereas, more often than not, this superabundant praise, on the part of those who mouth it, means, in reality, not that they believe the work to be of high worth, in itself, by any standards, but that they are surprised that it should come from Africa. Fulsome praise, the blaze of publicity, exciting and harmless as they may look, can do untold, even irreparable, harm to the up-coming intellectual: like sweet, seductive wine they can easily go to the head of the young, the immature, the unwary and the prone to pride; and thus blight a talent in the bud and ruin a life of promise. For once the intellectual ceases to think of himself as a humble

---

25. John Henry Cardinal Newman: *On the Scope and Nature of University Education*, Everyman's Library, pp. 9, 13-14.

seeker of the Truth in the vast unknown and assumes the airs of an omniscient demigod, the knell of his creative life begins to toll.

Next comes the attitude of those who appreciate the intrinsic worth of the genuine intellectual but shrewdly seek to use him, as a cat's paw, to achieve their own ends. This is very dangerous indeed; for if those who *seek to use him are men devoid of conscience,* men who know no scruples, men with covert or overt crooked intentions; and, if the intellectual thus enmeshed is spineless, or if he harbours a lurking appetite for material gain and preferment, he will surely end up by prostituting his talent and himself, and, thus, become a byword and a fraud. Indeed, if there is one thing we should ever keep in mind, it is that intellectualism, however high it towers, is no bulwark against human frailty. The higher it soars, the more shattering can be its fall.

Next come those, especially in positions of power, who affect the attitude that intellectuals count for nothing and can be dispensed with in the running of public affairs. Where this attitude becomes ingrained and general, it leads headlong (surely never to the weal but) to the woe of the commonwealth. You cannot banish mind from the running of the state and have it good.

Then comes that attitude prevalent, about a decade or two ago, in the USA where dedication to thought was looked upon with contempt, by a dollar-worshipping, materialist, action-crazy society for which achievement in the field of wealth was the highest good, as a bootless, worthless, if not despicable pursuit. It was the society which gave to the intellectual the scornful name of egg-head. In this mocking, disdainful atmosphere, it was only the intellectual firm in faith in the overwhelming need for intellectual enterprise, confident in its future and sure to be vindicated in the end, that could hold his head high amidst the jeering crowd. The unsure, the sensitive and cowardly were tempted to hide or to apologize for their existence. In those days, in the United States, a chap with a Harvard-Oxford back-ground who dared to run for Senate or Congress was a loser from the start. It took the shock of the first Soviet Spuntnik to jolt the Americans out of this senseless attitude. And lo! today, in the USA, the intellectual has come to his own, is being sought and wooed. Since, the days of President Kennedy, he is everywhere without the groves of academe: you find him in research, you find him in industry, you find him in places close to summit power, often not merely as a *back-room boy* but as an active participant on his own right deeply committed and involved. As I am writing this, the second pair of American astronauts are walking the moon.* The conquest of space (albeit by borrowed German brains) is ample evidence that the acceptance of the intellectual, in the United States, has paid enormous dividends and promises more untold.

We come now to the worst attitude of all. It is that which prevails where the intellectual has to seal his lips and live in dread of what might happen to him if he dares to speak his mind; where he has to face not merely 'the frown of the great' but is often the victim of fierce and cruel persecution. You found it, and find it still, where iron dictatorships of right or left have seized the state. Those of us who have lived through the last forty years, have seen some frightful things - Hitler's Germany, Stalin's Russia, Mussolini's Italy, McCarthy's witch-hunting in the United States. These are living memories. Khruschev's historic denunciation of Stalin in 1956 was an open avowal of this situation; and the Russian writers languishing in jail today are living evidence that in communist countries we have not seen the last of this state of things.

---

* Publisher's Note: The author is talking about the successful landing on the moon of Appolo 11 on July 20, 1969 with Astronauts Neil Armstrong and Edwin Aldrin, Jr.

Ideas are the most powerful things in the world, the most necessary and the most precious too; for any human achievement, however immense, however spectacular, however spell-binding, must, inevitably, take birth as an imponderable concept in a human mind. Consequently, thinking is the most necessary, the most noble activity of man. Indeed, it is, unquestionably, thanks to ceaseless thought that the world grows and develops and reshapes itself. Therefore, those in power who strive to suppress thought, whatever degree, for whatever reason, however see-mingly plausible, may be depriving the world of untold benefit: they thus can do irreparable harm and render themselves guilty, beyond pardon, of a heinous crime against humanity. Yes, it has happened before. Our concern is that nowhere on this earth, should it ever happen again.

Viewing society ceaselessly with a critical eye, the relentless scrutiny of the status quo, the endless questioning of the Establishment is a thing absolutely essential for the salutary renewal, for the continuous health, for the wholesome growth and vigour of the body politic. For, the human mind is imperfect and all its efforts and its creations, *ipso facto,* are imperfect; the human will is weak and that it should falter, that is should fail, that it should err, is rather in the nature of things, – should be expected as a matter of course. Even if an all-knowing, never-erring God elaborated an all-perfect system for society and handed it to man, man, unfailingly would taint it, would vitiate, at least its application, if not its very essence; because human nature, even where men dedicate themselves whole-heartedly to the search for goodness, to the attainment of perfection, remains corrupt, incurably.

Therefore, no system on this earth is sacrosanct, nothing that is the work of man lies untouchably without the bounds of criticisms.

The genuine thinker-scholar, more the less, con-scious of the limits of his mind, conscious of the frailty of his own will, will never be haughty, aloof and captious. On the contrary, he will be animated by sympathetic understanding, will encourage, support and praise the worthy efforts of public men in the bewildering, dangerous, care-vexing, health-consuming, thankless job of the running of the state. Yet he cannot cease to keep a critical eye on society; he cannot become purely and simply the poet laureate of the established system.

No thinker-scholar worthy of the name will even be tempted to degenerate into a rabble-rousing demagogue; into a perverted genius seeking to pull down where others strive to build; for thought, normally, does not develop in the crowd, in the market place, nor on the soap-box, nor in perverse scheming and intrigue. It germinates and grows in seclusion, in research and meditation, in a mind not merely fertile but also steeped in intellectual honesty.

What office-holders and wielders of power should look for in the intellectual is whether he has a deep education, a lucid mind pregnant with sound ideas; whether he is an assiduous gatherer of pertinent facts, a disinterested, dispassionate, impartial analyser and evaluator, a cold logician; whether his sincerity is transparent, his honesty above question, his will inflexible in the right; whether he is deeply and singleheartedly concerned about the public good. Once these things are sure, he should be given a hearing however unpalatable his conclusions may be.

No policy can be more short-sighted, more senseless, indeed more cruel and criminal than to silence men of thought, to fill them with affright, to make them live in anguish, or languish behind bars.

It is deep and far-sighted wisdom, on the part of rulers, to accept criticism and dissent as rather in the nature of things, as genuine signs of a healthy state. Indeed it should be cause for disquiet and concern to them, if nay-saying vanishes from public dialogue and debate. If they are hostile to criticism, avid for praise., they are soon surrounded by yes-men and sycophants, cringing fawning flatterers, who deceive them, who laud their thoughtless policies, who encourage them in wrong-headed waywardness, who urge them on to ruin in the end, and abandon them therein.

What then is the right policy, on the part of rulers, towards the intellectual?

The answer is simple and clear, as plain as a pike-staff: freedom; freedom from fear; freedom to follow his thought, without let or hindrance, to its logical end; freedom to say it as it is.

Once in liberal mood Mao cried: 'Let a hundred, flowers blossom, a hundred schools of thought content.' It may be argued that Mao, with his Cultural Revolution and his swarming hordes of Red Guards allowed neither a hundred schools of thought to sprout nor a hundred flowers to bloom. But that is beside the point; for the fact remains, notwithstanding, that in this acstatic outburst, in so far as the attitude of those in power towards intellectual enterprise is concerned. Mao gave voice to a policy that is sane, sober, sound, sagacious; indeed, the only one that is right.

Plato, as far back as twenty-two hundred years ago stressed the same point with more philosophic serenity:

> When the Persians, under Cyrus, he said, maintained the due balance between .slavery and freedom, they became, first of all, free themselves, and, after that, masters of many others. For when the rulers gave a share of freedom to their subjects and advanced them to a position of equality, the soldiers were more friendly towards their officers and showed their devotion in times of danger; and if there was any wise man amongst them, able to give counsel, since the king was not jealous but allowed free speech and respected those who could help at all by their counsel,

> – such a man had the opportunity of contributing to the common stock the fruit of his wisdom. Consequently, at that time all their affairs made progress, owing to their freedom, friendliness and mutual interchange of reason.[26]

In this treatise on the Nature, the End and the Purpose of University Studies, I may appear to have set goals too lofty to be achieved, standards too hard to be attained by a humanity imperfect in mind, weak of will, dominated by emotion, vexed by a thousand cares and fears, and plagued relentlessly by problems of livelihood and security, in a precarious world. Yet 1 remain convinced that the principles I have laid down in these pages, .namely, the acquisition of knowledge scientifically and philosophically profound, the cultivation of minds instilled with an instinctive, scientific and philosophical approach to all questions with which they are confronted, the forgoing of wills dead to private interest, but alive and fervently dedicated to the public service, of character courageous enough to become trusty, intrepid Keepers of the Public Conscience – I remain convinced, I say, that these principles enter into the very essence and substance of the Nature, the "End and the Purpose of University Studies.

I firmly believe, therefore, and profess that the inculcation of these ideals, from first to last, should remain the foremost preoccupation and duty of that Institution, whose very *raison d'être*, since its birth, has been the initiation of youth into intellectual enterprise, the steeling of wills in the unswerving choice of right, the furtherance of the growth of budding talents by urging them ever to pursue unrelentingly, the higher things of mind, the nobler aims of man, the loftier ends of life.

---

26. Plato: *The Laws*, Book III; The Loeb Classical Library Vol. 7. p. 225.

Chapter Nine

Tributes to Professor Dr. Bernard Fonlon (19ᵗʰ November 1924 – 26ᵗʰ August 1986)

Remembering Dr. Bernard Fonlon
By Paul Verdzekov – Archbishop Emeritus of Bamenda (Originally published in 2006 on the 20th anniversary of Dr. Fonlon's passing)

1. Twenty years ago, on 26th August 1986, Bernard Nsokika Fonlon died in Canada. He had gone there in the month of May of that year in order to receive a doctorate degree in Literature (D. Litt.) from the University of Guelph, and it was his intention to spend the 1986/1987 academic year in the United States of America, within the framework of a Fulbright programme. But the Lord, the Giver of Life, decided otherwise. Bernard died in Canada at the age of sixty-one years, and nine months and six days. He would have been sixty-two years of age on 19th November 1986.

His mortal remains were brought home to Cameroon, and he was buried behind Saint Teresa's Cathedral at Kimbo', in the Nso' country, the little town where he was born on 19th November 1924. The mortal remains of Bernard Fonlon arrived back in Cameroon at the time when the people of Cameroon, as a whole, and of the Bamenda Grasslands, in particular, were devastated by a sudden and unexpected tragedy, namely, the Lake Nyos gas disaster, which occurred on 21st August 1986, and which, within minutes, claimed the lives of hundreds and hundreds of our fellow country men and women.

2. In an Obituary written for the Summer 1986 issue of the Bulletin of the *African Literature Association*, Edmonton, Canada, *I.C. Tcheho*, of the University of Yaounde, said, inter alia:

"Throughout all his life, he (Professor Fonlon) was the very incarnation of his belief in the supremacy of intellectual life over the material life. Consequently, he practised, in a rare manner, the virtue of detachment from materialist preoccupations. 'I have not garnered gold', he writes with emphasis in a second Letter addressed to the Bishops of Buea and Bamenda in 1979...

By means of a great number of his everyday life, Bernard Nsokika Fonlon fought hard, without counting the cost, for the triumph, here and now, of the essential values of the human being. In a very special manner, he was preoccupied in the highest degree by the future of African Youth in contemporary Africa which is extremely exposed to moral degradation. He held that every African, whatever be his or her position of responsibility, has the sacred duty to seek excellence at all times...

The moral ideal of Bernard Fonlon can be summed up in that other adage which he liked to cite in learned Latin: *Integer vitae scelerisque purus* (Purity of a life untarnished by sin)" (My weak and approximate translation from the French original).

3. Another Obituary by a close friend of Bernard Fonlon, which also appeared in the above-mentioned bulletin of the *African Literature Association*, is that of *Richard Bjornson* of Ohio State University. He said, inter alia:

"The death of Bernard Fonlon in an Ottawa hospital room was completely overshadowed by the horror of the Lake Nyos disaster that occurred some thirty miles from his birthplace of Banso in the North-West Province of Cameroon. In some ways, the very fact that he died in semi-obscurity is symbolically appropriate, for despite the accomplishments of his life, Fonlon was a humble man, who never really sought the limelight. As others gained fame and notoriety, he laboured patiently and effectively – as a government minister, as the editor of an impressive cultural journal, and as a teacher – to realize the lofty ideals he had set for himself. He always defended the highest standards of excellence, and unlike many of his successful countrymen, he was never interested in amassing a personal fortune. In fact, he became an almost legendary exemplar of integrity and the modest life style in a country where conspicuous consumption is commonly regarded as a perquisite of success".

4. Another touching tribute to Bernard Nsokika Fonlon is that of his friend, *Professor G.D. Killam*, of *Guelph University*. His tribute to Bernard Fonlon also appears in the above-mentioned Bulletin of the African Literature Association, Edmonton. Professor Killam said, inter alia:

"Dr. Bernard Fonlon's contribution to Cameroonian life in politics and education is salutary and will remain so. He held important ministries and built for Cameroon an airline and telecommunication network, a public transport service, a health and welfare system – all of which make a proud legacy. His tireless effort in securing the reputation of the Department of African Literature, the only such Department in the world, adds to the uniqueness of Dr. Fonlon's career and further establishes his vision. He had an impressive number of 'firsts': he was the first Cameroonian to receive a Ph.D. and he directed the first Ph.D. thesis in Cameroon. He was the first Cameroonian to receive national honours in Nigeria, Germany and Tunisia, and he was proud of the fact that the D. Litt. bestowed on him by the University of Guelph in 1986 was the first to be received by a Cameroonian, and it was the one he most cherished.

All these achievements are well documented. Dr. Fonlon's spirit will move through Cameroon after his death as it did when he was alive".

5. That Bernard Fonlon's spirit would "move through Cameroon after his death as it did when he was alive", (dixit Professor Killam), was also affirmed by some students of the University of Yaounde in a tribute published in the Government-owned newspaper, *Cameroon Tribune*, very shortly after Bernard's death and burial. Among the many concrete examples of a life of unimpeachable integrity which, according to the students, Bernard Fonlon leaves as a legacy to the youth of this country, they singled one for special mention, and which I cite from memory. After his retirement as Professor from the University of Yaounde, the students wrote that Bernard Fonlon continue to direct their theses, dissertations and 'memoires' completely freely, not seeking, or asking for, or expecting, any fees, offerings or inducements (the so-called 'motivations') of any kind. His only joy and satisfaction in this regard was to see young Cameroonians contributing to the advancement of knowledge. The students of the University of Yaounde said that they most deeply appreciated Bernard Fonlon for this action.

6. Professor Killam's conviction that Bernard Fonlon's spirit "will move through Cameroon after his death as it did when he was alive" is also illustrated by a paper celebrating Professor Fonlon's legacy presented by *Eugene Nyuydine Ngalim* on the occasion of the celebration of the nineteenth anniversary of Bernard's death held at Yaounde on 24th November 2005. Eugene Nyuydine presented that Paper on behalf of the *Cameroon Youths and Students Forum for Peace*.

In his own paper entitled: *Remembering Dr. Bernard Fonlon*, *William Tallah* said, inter alia, on the same occasion:

'Eugene was still in Primary School when Dr. Fonlon died in 1986. Like many young people of today, Eugene never met Dr. Fonlon, yet the passion and drive with which he went about gathering the interviews on Dr. Fonlon for this occasion is unparalleled".

Eugene Nyuydine Ngalim's paper, his activities and those of his friends for the celebration of last November is a sign that the legacy left by Bernard Fonlon to the Youth of this country is alive.

7. When I revisited the book entitled *Socrates in Cameroon*, a University of Yaounde Publication edited by *Nalova Lyonga* and published by Tortoise Books in 1989, I was struck by the following Reflections in the Churchyard of Kumbo Cathedral, 27th February 1988, by Professor **Victor Anomah Ngu**;

Bernard Fonlon, M.A., Ph.D., (Nui) Dip. Ed. (Oxon), Professor, born 19 November 1924, died 26 August1986. That is what was printed on Bernard Fonlon's tombstone. That is what he was called when he lived with us until that fateful but happy day in August 1986, when Ben left us for another world.

But what do they call him now, up there where all good men and women go? If you were to go there and ask for a certain Professor Fonlon, M.A., Ph.D., they would probably simply laugh at you. Such titles mean nothing there.

Why did God call Bernard Fonlon before he came into our world on 19 November 1924? Since God knows each one of His creatures, he had a name before he was baptized Bernard. And now that he has returned to his permanent heavenly home, he will take up his real name once again. It would not include such empty and pompous titles and degrees as Professor or Ph. D. Nor for that matter are there any Excellencies, Majesties, Graces, Eminences, or Holinesses there in heaven either. The names and tittles we bear here on earth we must bear lightly indeed, like the numbers jockeys bear on their backs when they ride in a race and which they must set aside when they go home at the end of the race.

Our real names and our real titles await us when we join Bernard Fonlon. WE will find, if we are lucky enough to join Bernard Fonlon, that he is not a Ph. D. but a BMH, MCPG, Beloved of the Most High, or Member of the Celestial Philosophical Group of which Newman will almost certainly be a member..." (*Socrates in Cameroon*, pp. 159-160).

These Reflections of Professor Anomah Ngu remind us of the following words of the Congregation for the Doctrine of the Faith on the Question of Admission of Women to the Ministerial Priesthood:

"The Church is a differentiated body, in which each individual has a role; the tasks are distinct, and must not be confused; they do not favour the superiority of one over the other, nor do they provide an excuse for jealousy; the only better gift, which can and must be desired is love (cf. 1 Cor 12-13). The greatest in the kingdom of heaven are not the ministers but the saints" (*Inter Insigniores*, n. 6).

8. In the course of 1953, when he was a third year student of Theology at Bigard Memorial Seminary, Enugu, Bernard wrote a poem entitled: *To A Departed Master's Memory*. It was a poem in memory of *Father Thomas Burke Kennedy*, an Irish Mill Hill Missionary, who taught Bernard in Sacred Heart Primary School, Shisong, in the nineteen thirties, and who had a decisive and lasting formative influence on him. Father Kennedy died at Njinikom in 1953, and is buried there. Bernard had intended publishing that poem, together with other articles, on the occasion of his ordination to the Priesthood, which was expected to take place in 1954. However, "on the very eve of the Final Step, the Subdiaconate, six months away from the Priesthood, my

life took a sharp and unexpected turn. And my day of triumph never came!" (Bernard Fonlon). As he himself used to put it in his usual blunt and matter-of-fact manner, he was "dismissed" from the Seminary.

Seventeen years later, towards the end of 1969, Bernard sent that poem to me, together with other articles making up a pamphlet entitled: *As I see it,* for serialization in a monthly of the Diocese of Buea, *Cameroon Panorama*. With specific reference to the poem, he wrote inter alia, on 24th December 1969:

"Today, I have decided to publish it exactly as it was written. I do so in the hope that, imperfect though it be as a matter of course, it will, nevertheless, recall a worthy man, and a worthy priest; and arouse the tribute of prayer in the hearts of those who loved him. I do so in the hope that it will enkindle, even for a moment, the sorrowful memory of Father Burke Kennedy".

9. On this occasion of the twentieth anniversary of Bernard's death, one would like to borrow his mournful words about that Irish Mill Hill Missionary, who was his hero, by expressing the hope that the foregoing lines will, somehow, "arouse the tribute of a prayer in the hearts of those who loved" Bernard Fonlon. May these lines help to "enkindle, even for a moment, the sorrowful memory" of Bernard.

Christian Cardinal Tumi on Bernard Fonlon

Opening remarks by His Eminence Christian Cardinal Tumi, Archbishop of Douala, on the occasion of the celebration of the 19th anniversary of the death of Professor Bernard Nsokika Fonlon.

Distinguished guests Ladies and Gentlemen:

When the organizers of this evening asked me to chair this occasion, I did not hesitate at all to say: "Yes, I will be there with you!" Why? Because this event brings to mind many memories of a truly great Cameroonian, a truly great statesman, a truly great Christian, in short, a truly great human being: Dr. Bernard Nsokika Fonlon.

For you to have thought of dedicating a whole evening to Bernard's memory is really wonderful and I thank you for it. I know many of the speakers we have this evening will have much to say about this great son of our land; so I will be brief in my own remarks.

My memory of Dr. Fonlon goes back to when I was still a child. I was in the vernacular school in my village of Kikaikelaki when he came to teach there after completing Standard Six. In fact, it is he who, a year later, closed the vernacular school and moved all of us to Shisong, where we started our primary education in English.

He was, of course, a role model for us. We were all fascinated by this very simple, young and friendly man with an easy smile, who liked to spend a good part of his time in the presence of older people. He would listen attentively to them and ask them questions from time to time. His spirit of inquiry, the inquisitiveness of an intellectual mind, was already at work in him.

Our mothers always prepared food for him, which we took to him and he would always invite us to join him, so we ate it together. As a child, being asked by a teacher to share his meal was always something that left an indelible mark on your memory.

He didn't wear any shoes but I remember that when he bought his first pair of shoes, his mother was very furious with him. Her fear was simply that he might start to become too proud and would not listen to his parents and the elders of society anymore. Of course, she didn't have to worry at all for Bernard remained the obedient young man he had always been.

Some years later, he left for Saint Charles College in Onitsha, Nigeria, to prepare for the priesthood. For quite some years thereafter, I didn't see him, nor heard from or about him. But then, one day, some friends and I were playing football in a field near the warders' barracks at the Bamenda Station when we saw him coming. I immediately recognized him and hid behind a shrub until he came nearer and then I jumped out and held him. Once he overcame that moment of surprise, and realizing who I was, he screamed out "Shaghan, what are you doing here?" And that was a moment of joy for both of us. Our encounters in later years would always be marked by great joy.

Bernard was a very approachable man. He loved to play the flute and we always loved listening to him play it. My love of music certainly received a big boost from his own musical talents.

When we learnt that he had been asked to leave the Seminary, we were all profoundly shaken. We later learnt that he was told a few days to his diaconal ordination that he would not be ordained a deacon. And to tell you the kind of man he was, it was he who played the organ in Church a few days later when his classmates were being ordained deacons! I wonder how many of us would have even attended that ordination Mass, not to mention playing the organ!

But that was the type of man Bernard was. A truly humble man, a man of discipline, a man of principles, a man of prayers, a man who loved the truth, a man who had great respect for the views of others, even those he did not share. A man of deep conviction. A man young people should truly admire and imitate and I am happy that you've organized an evening in his honour so the younger generation may emulate those values for which he stood so firmly. He was an intellectual of the first order. A man who loved work well done and who took his time to do work well. Our younger ones can learn much from his example.

As you all know, I'm not the only one who fell, as it were, under Bernard's spell. The Archbishop of Bamenda, His Grace Paul Verdzekov, was also like his godson. Many other bishops and priests of our land benefited enormously from his wise pieces of advice and encouragement. It is thanks to him, and other lay faithful of like mind and commitment to the Church, that we have the Saint Thomas Aquinas Major Seminary in Bambui, that has given our country so many priests since its creation.

I mentioned that he was a man of prayer, and indeed he was! Instead of revolting against the Church in bitterness for not being ordained a priest, as many in his place might have been tempted to do, he instead accepted what had happened to him and continued to play a prominent role in church as a lay person.

He was indeed a saintly man. When I was in Rome recently, a Nigerian Cardinal, who had known Bernard when he was studying in Nigeria, asked me why we have not yet introduced his cause for beatification. That is how strongly people even outside our country consider him worthy of being declared a Saint.

Many gathered here this evening will have much more to say about this man of fortitude, of temperance and of prudence. Once more, thank you for making me a part of this memorial occasion. God bless you.

Bernard Fonlon: In Memoriam

By Richard Bjornson, The Ohio State University

The death of Bernard Fonlon in an Ottawa room was completely overshadowed by the horror of the Lake Nyos disaster that occurred some thirty miles from his birthplace of Banso in the North-West Province of Cameroon. In some way, the very fact that he died in semi-obscurity is symbolically appropriate, for despite the accomplishments of his life, Fonlon was a humble man, who never really sought the limelight.

As others gained fame and notoriety, he laboured patiently and effectively – as a government minister, as the editor of an impressive cultural journal, and as a teacher – to realize the lofty ideals he had ser for himself. He always defended the highest standards of excellence, and unlike many of his successful countrymen, he was never interested in amassing a personal fortune. In fact, he became an almost legendary exemplar of integrity and the modest life style in a country where conspicuous consumption is commonly regarded as a perquisite of success. Strangers who met Fonlon for the first time during the final decade of his life were not always immediately impressed with him. He was often drowsy. He tended to ramble. His opinion on most subjects had been formed years ago and seemed to resist change. Younger students complained that he had not kept pace with recent developments in African literature, and even his best friends had to exercise patience when he launched into the endless retelling of anecdotes from his past.

Nevertheless, few people ever met Fonlon without sensing that there was something more – something profoundly human – behind the avuncular stolidity of his manner. Perhaps it was a playful glint in his eye; perhaps it was a burst of impassioned rhetoric; perhaps it was the quiet wisdom of a man who, having imbibed deeply from many cultures, continued to believe that human dignity was possible in a chaotic and corrupt world. Whatever it was, this intangible quality made people aware that Bernard Fonlon was a presence. What many people did not realize was that he had been seriously injured in an automobile accident during the early 1970s. He lay in a coma for over a week at that time. He almost died. Afterwards he frequently complained of headaches, and the medicines he took to relieve the pain impaired his ability to concentrate. He felt tired, and he began to hope aloud that a younger generation of Cameroonians would assume some of the responsibilities he had for so long taken upon himself. The journal Abbia, which he had worked so hard to keep afloat for over twenty years, floundered and finally ceased publication. His lectures at the university became sporadic.

Nevertheless, people continued to admire him, for they could feel the spark of humanity in him. It was this spark that enabled him to respond with enthusiasm to the teachings of a Catholic missionary in Banso more than fifty years ago; in fact, much of his subsequent life makes sense in terms of the moral idealism he absorbed from Father Kennedy. The same spark gave him the courage to walk for weeks through the tropical rain forest to enrol in the seminary at Onitsha. It also gave him the courage to write an open letter to the bishop, pointing out ways in which African priests were treated less well than their European counterparts. This letter brought about his expulsion from the seminary three weeks before his scheduled ordination.

Yet, despite the racism of the colonial church, Fonlon never confused the ideals of Christianity with the practices of its corrupt adherents. The spark of humanity in him continued to inspire his efforts as he taught school in Nigeria, obtained his doctorate in Ireland (with one of the first dissertations on the awakening of the black consciousness), served the young Ahidjo government in many capacities (including that of gadfly and moral conscience), and taught the black literature he passionately loved. During all this time, Fonlon wrote poetry, essays about civic responsibility, editorials about the appreciation of literature, papers about bilingual education, speeches about political reconciliation. Much of his writing has been reprinted, although it has never been collected and edited in such a way as to reveal the genuine contributions he made to his country and to African letters. Fonlon accomplished a great deal during his lifetime, and he set a high standard for others to follow.

Although his greatest influence was undoubtedly on the lives of his fellow countrymen, he touched nearly everyone in important ways because that spark of humanity always glowed in him. He loved the region around Banso and always remained deeply attached to the culture of his people. At the same time, he opened himself to other cultures, and he committed himself unreservedly to the ideal of a unified Cameroon. His presence will be missed, and it is unfortunate that he never completed the memoirs upon which he was working at the moment of his death. With him died a great deal of knowledge, experience, and wisdom that might have been shared with others through the pages of his projected book. Bernard was a good writer, a good teacher, and a good statesman, but he was above all a good man.

Remembering Bernard Fonlon

By G. D. Killam, University of Guelph

Dr Bernard Fonlon's contribution to Cameroonian life in politics and education is salutary and will remain so. He held important ministries and built for Cameroon an airlines and telecommunications network, a public transport service, a health and welfare system – all of which make a proud legacy. His tireless effort in securing the reputation of the Department of African Literature, the only such Department in the world, adds to the uniqueness of Dr. Fonlon's career and further establishes his vision.

He had an impressive number of "firsts": he was the first Cameroonian to receive a Ph.D., and he directed the first Ph.D. thesis within Cameroon. He was the first Cameroonian to receive national honours in Nigeria, Germany and Tunisia and he was proud of the fact that the D.Litt. bestowed upon him by the University of Guelph in 1986 was the first received by a Cameroonian, and was the one he most cherished. All these achievements are well documented. Dr. Fonlon's spirit will move through Cameroon after his death as it did when he was alive - he was "doctor", "professor" and his voice rang with the humanity of his soul throughout Cameroon.

But it is the personal loss that one feels that possesses one at this time. He was a close, personal friend and colleague and our collaboration on various ventures over the past five years not only brought us close together but revealed a common sympathy of purpose and understanding. We travelled together in Cameroon and found our time comfortably spent in the discussion of a wide range of literary and cultural matters and I found myself, as it were, a learner at his feet. It was not for nothing that he was described as "the Socrates of Africa". His hopes for the country, revealed in his untiring work on its behalf, reflect his faith in the Socratic method. More than that, it is at a time like this when he is dead - too young at sixty-one years – that the little unremembered acts of kindness and consideration and courtesy are once again remembered. These provide both a strong sense of loss and grief and at the same time promise a consolation for the future in remembering him and his affection.

Bernard Fonlon of Nso : The Pathfinder

By Professor Aliko Songolo, University of California – Irvine

The news of Bernard Fonlon's death reached me as Cameroon was mourning the more than 1700 deaths of the tragedy of lake Nyos, in his region of origin. He died in far away Canada, unable to be with his countrymen in their hour of sorrow.

Bernard Fonlon of Nso was a worthy son of Cameroon. He was one of the early intellectuals who aspired to shape the destiny of their country and that of the African continent. For a quarter of a century, he served his people in various capacities: several times as minister in the government at critical moments in the history of Cameroon, and later as Professor and Head of the Department of African Literature, where he contributed mightily in shaping young minds for the future of Cameroon. It was during the last two years of his distinguished career that I had the privilege to know him and to work with him. He was a leader. He led by example. For every collective undertaking, he led by formulating ideas and by establishing attainable goals. He listened carefully to his collaborators' points of view and then charted the course to follow. As he was bored by details, he gave to others the opportunity to implement his ideas.

Though he was in politics, he was not a politician: he was more interested in the res publica, that is, the state as a communal endeavour. In short, Bernard Fonlon was a statesman in the best sense of the word: he believed in public service with selfless dedication and unwavering integrity. Bernard Fonlon of Nso was a learned man. Like a Renaissance man, he sought to know everything there is to know on a given subject. He believed that every intellectual question has its "fundamental principles." He was educated in the classical mould of Europe, yet he remained close to home in his daily life. On his weekly radio show, "The Classical Hour," he surprised many a listener by introducing West African Highlife alongside Mozart and Beethoven. Bernard Fonlon of Nso was above all a man of compassion and a man of humility.

He took personal interest in the welfare of others. He took the time to help the helpless and to comfort the bereaved. He eschewed the trappings and pomposity of high office and title to live like the people, to be with the people. He has left behind sons and daughters he never had, brothers and sisters whose lives he touched in countless and untold ways. Bernard Fonlon of Nso: a cultured man, a compassionate man of the people, a friend.

Nécrologie : Bernard Fonlon n'est plus

Par I. C. Tcheo, Université de Yaoundé

La pénible réalité : le 27 août 1986, Shu Faî Docteur Bernard Nsokika Fonlon a rendu l'âme dans un hôpital à Ottawa, au Canada. Il avait quitté le Cameroun au début du mois de mai 1986, pour aller recevoir un D.Lit. à l'Université de Guelph. Il se proposait de passer, par la suite, l'année académique 86/87 aux Etats-Unis, dans le cadre d'un programme Fulbright. Mais la mort ne lui donnera pas l'occasion de réaliser ce projet. Elle l'a surpris en pleine activité et, désormais, nous ne parlerons plus de Bernard Fonlon qu'au passé.

La dernière impression qu'il laisse, dans ces conditions, est celle d'un travailleur acharné, constamment absorbé par un programme immense d'activité intellectuelles. Cette image est bien celle be Bernard Fonlon, ce penseur qui a affirmé dans un de ses écrits : « Ideas are the most important things in the world. » Toute sa vie durant, il a effectivement incarné la croyance en la suprématie de la vie intellectuelle sur la vie matérielle. D'où, chez lui, la pratique peu commune du détachement des préoccupations matérialistes. « I have not garnered gold, »' (je n'ai pas amassé d'or) écrit-il avec emphase dans une deuxième lettre ouverte adressée aux Evêques de Buéa et Bamenda en 1979. Les soixante deux années de sa vie ont été des années d'abnégation, de tension vers un idéal intellectuel, de pratique d'une éthique faite d'ascèse mais gouvernée par l'humanisme le plus détaché q'un homme de ma connaissance ait incarné avec bonheur. Ces qualités étaient en harmonie avec l'humilité légendaire du pédagogue émérite qu'était en même temps le Professor Fonlon.

History of The Fonlon-Nichols Award

Bernard FONLON was a teacher, writer, editor of literary journals, and head of the African Literature Department at the University of Yaoundé. He passionately defended human rights in an often oppressive political atmosphere. When this noted Cameroonian man of letters died in 1986, a group of his friends from around the world decided to seek an appropriate way of honouring his memory.

Mobilized largely by Stephen Arnold (then Director of the Research Institute for African and Caribbean Literature – RICLAC – at the University of Alberta), these friends of

Bernard Fonlon contributed to a memorial fund in his name. These contributions were matched by the Provincial Government of Alberta (Canada).

At about this time Lee NICHOLS announced his retirement. Nichols is a journalist whose positions in support of human rights and against racism are especially known among scholars of African literature for his historic Voice of America reports on the development of African literatures from the sixties to the present.

The executive committee of RICLAC felt it would be appropriate to associate his name to that of Bernard Fonlon, both having shared a commitment to democratic ideals, humanistic values, and literary excellence in Africa.

At its 1993 meeting in Guadeloupe, the Executive of the African Literature Association resolved that the Award be conferred regularly at the annual meetings of the ALA.

The Fonlon-Nichols Award is given every year to an African writer for excellence in creative writing and for contributions to the struggles for human rights and freedom of expression

http://www.arts.ualberta.ca/%7Echinook/fonlon-nichols/

Bernard Fonlon: A Select Bibliography

This section will contain a select bibliography of all publications by and about Dr. Bernard Fonlon. The current bibliography is not an exhaustive one. Tracking down publications by Fonlon has been a Herculean task since virtually all of his works are currently out of print. The same is the case with most of the books about his life and philosophy which were limited edition releases in Cameroon. It is our hope that the public will help in updating the current bibliographical selection, and if possible, make available copies of his out of print works.

Books and Articles by Bernard Fonlon

FONLON, Bernard. (1998). *An open letter to the bishops of Buea and Bamenda*. Published (25 years after) on the occasion of the silver jubilee of the foundation of St. Thomas Aquinas' Major Seminary, Bambui. 68 p.

FONLON, Bernard. "Upon Rock or upon Sand" in Lyonga, Nalova (ed.). (1989). *Socrates in Cameroon. The Life and Works of Bernard Fonlon*. Yaounde, Leeds: Tortoise Books.

FONLON, Bernard. 1983. *A simple story simply told: or the rise of Dr. Pavel Verkovsky, First Archbishop of Bamenda*. 51 p.

FONLON, Bernard.(1982). *ABBIA* nos. 38-39-40.

FONLON, Bernard. 1978. Lettre *ouverte aux étudiants africains, ou, La nature, la fin et le but des études universitaires*. Yaounde, Cameroon: University of Cameroon.

FONLON, Bernard. *La Poésie et le réveil de l'homme noir*. Kinshasa: Presses de l'université du Zaire, 1978.

FONLON, Bernard. "The language problem in Cameroon: an historical perspective". In David R Smock; Kwamena Bentsi-Enchill (eds). *The Search for national integration in Africa*. New York: Free Press, 1976.

FONLON, Bernard. (1973). *An Open Letter to the Bishops of Buea and Bamenda*. Yaounde.

FONLON, Bernard (1978): *The genuine intellectual*. Buma Kor publishing house Yaounde

FONLON, Bernard. 1977. *Education through literature: a paper*.

FONLON, Bernard. (1973). *Random Leaves from my Diary*. Buea : Catholic Press.

FONLON, Bernard 1970s. *Flaubert, écrivain*. 92 leaves.

FONLON, Bernard. *Culture et acculturation (Point de vue, 12)*. Yaoundé, Clé, 1972.

FONLON, Bernard. 1971. *As I see it*. Yaounde, Cameroon: Catholic Press. 71 p.

FONLON, Bernard. 1969 / 1971. *To every African freshman: or, the nature, end and purpose of university studies*. ABBIA 23-24-26. Victoria: Cameroon Times Press. 100 p.

FONLON, Bernard (1969) "The Language Problem in Cameroon: A Historical Perspective" in *ABBIA* 22, pp. 5-40.

FONLON, Bernard. (1968) "Idea of cultural Integration", in *ABBIA* n.20, 5-29.

FONLON, Bernard. (1966). *The Task of Today*. Victoria, Cameroon: Cameroon Printing and Publishing company Ltd.

FONLON, Bernard. "Idea of Culture - Le concept de la culture", in *ABBIA* (1965) n.11, 5-29, 31-38; (1967) n.16, 5-24; (1968) n.19, 5-29.

FONLON, Bernard. *To every son of Nso*. Yaoundé: CEPER, 1965.

FONLON, Bernard. "Under the Sign of Rising Sun". The *Cameroon Times*, 1965.

FONLON, Bernard. "A Case for an Early Bilingualism," *ABBIA*, No 4, 1963, 56-94.

FONLON, Bernard. "The Idea of Culture" *ABBIA* No. 2

FONLON, Bernard. 1963. "Inaugural Article". *ABBIA*, No. 1.

Interviews and Seminars

National Educational Television and Radio Center. *African Writers of Today*. Program Numbers 1-6. NY: c. 1964.

(Transcripts of a series of television programs featuring interviews with one or more African writers. Writers interviewed on these six programs were Amos Tutuola, Ulli Beier, David Rubadiri, Leopold Sedaar Senghor, **Bernard Fonlon**, Wole Soyinka, Ezekiel Mphahlele, Chinua Achebe and William Abraham.)

Conference of African Writers of English Expression. Convened by Mbari Writers' and Artists' Club (Ibadan, Nigeria) in Collaboration with the Department of Extra-Mural Studies, Makerere College. Sponsored by The Congress for Cultural Freedom. Kampala, Uganada: Makerere University College, 11-17 June, 1962. First edition, 120 pages.

(Contains discussion papers and reports by J. Saunders Redding, Ulli Beier, Ezekial Mphahlele, Arthur Drayton, Gerald Moore, Donatus Nwoga, Boke Modisane, Segun Olusola, J. P. Clark, Lewis Nkosi, **Bernard Fonlon** et al. The introduction states that this conference "was the first get-together of African authors writing in English anywhere in the world.")

Books and Articles on Fonlon

Chem-Langhee, Bongfen. *The Shuufaayship of Professor Bernard Nsokika Fonlon.* 1989 114p.
Krieger, Milton. "Building the Republic through Letters: Abbia: Cameroon Cultural Review, and its Legacy." *Research in African Literatures*, Vol. 27, No. 2, 1996. 155 – 177.
Lantum, Daniel. 1992. *Dr. Bernard Nsokika Fonlon, an intellectual in politics.* 80 p.
Lantum, Daniel. 1988. *Dr. Bernard Nsokika Fonlon, 1924-1986, is now a legend : funeral addresses, tributes, and eulogies.* Kumbo Town, Cameroon: NSO History Society, 107 p.
Lyonga, Nalova (ed.). *Socrates in Cameroon. The Life and Works of Bernard Fonlon,* Yaounde, Leeds: Tortoise Books, 1989)
Mbayu, Kevin (ed). 1994. *The moral question: a philosophical debate between Dr. Bernard Fonlon and Mr. Kevin Mbayu: including Random leaves from my diary and Thoughts for the time.* Cameroon: s.n., 238 p.
Mbunwe-Samba, Patrick. (1993). *Sixth anniversary of the death of Professor Bernard Nsokika Fonlon (1924-1986).* Bamenda: ACT (Association for Creative Teaching). 71 p.
Monono, Churchill Ewumbue. *The torch and the throne: The political philosophy of Bernard Fonlon.* Yaounde: Editions SOPECAM. 1991. 72 pages.
Ngwafor, E.N. (1989). *Law in Action: Five Sensitive Moot court Submissions Including tributes to Chief Justice S.M.L. Endeley and Professor Bernard Fonlon.* London: Institute of third World Art and Literature. 206 p.
Wambeng, Samuel N. & Patrick Mbunwe-Samba (eds.) (1988). *A Tribute to Professor Bernard Nsokika Fonlon, 1924-1986.* Bamenda, Cameroon: Association for Creative Teaching (ACT). 116 p.

www.ingramcontent.com/pod-product-compliance
Lightning Source LLC
Chambersburg PA
CBHW021832300426
44114CB00009BA/405